SENTENCED TO HELL

By the same author:

Eglwys Cyngar Sant Llangefni: guide book (English and Welsh)

Forty Years of Treading the Boards: a history of Theatr Fach, Llangefni (English and Welsh)

O Fôn i Van Diemen's Land

Melinau Môn

Sentenced to Hell

*The story of men and women
transported from north Wales,
1730-1878*

J. Richard Williams

First published in 2011

© J. Richard Williams

Copyright © by Llygad Gwalch 2010.
All rights reserved. No part of this publication
may be reproduced or transmitted, in any form   ·
or by any means, without permission.

ISBN: 978-1-84524-175-9

Cover design: Lynwen Jones

Published by
Llygad Gwalch, Ysgubor Plas, Llwyndyrys,
Pwllheli, Gwynedd, Wales, LL53 6NG.
Tel: 01758 750432
e-mail: books@carreg-gwalch.com
www.carreg-gwalch.com

Thanks to Mavis, my wife, for being so patient,
and to my late father, John Williams,
for awakening my interest in history,
and making me realise the importance of
the history of one's locality.

Convict Maid

Ye city maids, attend to me
While I relate my misery.
Through city streets I oft have strayed
But now I am a Convict Maid.

In innocence I once did live,
In all the joy that peace could give.
But sin my youthful heart betrayed,
And now I am a Convict Maid.

To wed my lover, I did try
To take my master's property,
So all my guilt was soon displayed,
And I became a Convict Maid.

Then I was soon to prison sent
To wait in fear my punishment,
When at the bar I stood dismayed
Since doomed to be a Convict Maid.

At length the judge did me address –
Which filled with pain my aching breast:
'To Botany Bay you will be conveyed,
for seven years a Convict Maid.'

For seven long years oh! how I sighed,
While my poor mother loudly cried.
My lover wept, and thus he said,
'May God be with my Convict Maid.'

To you that here my mournful take
I cannot half my grief reveal.
No sorrow yet has been portrayed
Like that of the poor Convict Maid.

Far from my friends and home so dear,
My punishment is most severe.
My woe is great, and I'm afraid
That I shall die a Convict Maid.

I toil each day in grief and pain,
And sleepless through the night remain.
My constant toils are unrepaid,
And wretched is the Convict Maid.

Oh could I but once more be free,
I'd never again a captive be,
But I would seek some honest trade
And never become a Convict Maid.

(Australian broadside ballad)

Contents

Foreword

Written history is at its most poignant when it documents the lives of ordinary people who became victims of social and political change. The crimes allegedly committed by the individuals who were unmercifully banished from north Wales to penal settlements in north America and Australia were, more often than not, petty, and motivated by dire poverty and human necessity.

It is a tragic and moving tale which, unfortunately, has been largely overlooked by modern Welsh historians.

Richard Williams, by recounting their plight, has made a significant contribution to our understanding of life in nineteenth-century north Wales. His thoroughly-researched work is a fitting memorial to the banished and, until the publication of this book, the forgotten.

Dr William R. Lewis
August 2010, Ynys Môn

Bibliography

Caernarvon & Denbigh Herald

Lewis Lloyd, *Australians from Wales* (Gwasanaeth Archifau Gwynedd, 1988)

Emlyn Richards, *Bywyd Gŵr Bonheddig* (Gwasg Gwynedd, 2002)

H. J. Owen, *From Merioneth to Botany Bay* (Bala, 1952)

Ioan Mai, *O Ben Llŷn i Botany Bay* (Llanrwst, 1993)

Coultman Smith, *Shadow over Tasmania* (J. Walch & Sons, 1941)

Charles Bateson, *The Convict Ships* (Brown, Son & Ferguson, 1959)

A Roger Ekirch, *Bound for America: the transportation of British convicts to the Colonies, 1718–1775* (Oxford, 1987)

Robert J. Brugger, *Maryland: a middle temperament, 1630–1980* (Baltimore, 1989)

Tom Keneally, *The Commonwealth of Thieves – The Story of the Founding of Australia* (Chatto and Windus, 2006)

A. Brooke and David Brandon, *Bound For Botany Bay – British Convict Voyages to Australia* (The National Archives, 2005)

Babette Smith, *Australia's Birthstain* (Allen and Unwin 2008)

'His Majesty's Colony of Van Diemen's Land is not intended to reform criminals, but simply to store them, like so much rubbish in a dust heap, so that England can be emptied of trouble makers once and for all.'

Matthew Kneale, *English Passengers*, 2002

Introduction

Wales has often been called *'Gwlad y Menig Gwynion'* – 'the Land/Country of White Gloves'. This refers to the tradition of the Judge wearing white gloves at the Assize Court – but only if there were no criminal cases before him. A report from the *Caernarvon and Denbigh Herald* on 29 July 1865 is sufficent explanation:

> The High Sheriff, addressing his Lordship, now said, 'As High Sheriff of this county, and there not being a single prisoner for trial, I have very great pleasure, in compliance with an ancient custom, and I consider it a privilege, to present you with a pair of white gloves . . . likewise the Judge's officers.'
>
> His Lordship returned thanks, saying they all knew well – and rejoiced in – the purity of the morals of the people of this county.

It is not known how many 'case free' assizes were held, but many prisoners from Wales were sent overseas after appearing in courts where 'white gloves' were *not* seen. No Welsh county can boast that no-one was transported from within its confines. Cardiganshire may have the best record in that only one of its female citizens was sent out to Australia, the unlucky lady being Eleanor James, who was sent out on the ship *Brothers* during September 1822 to Van Diemen's Land for seven years, but even she had the company of a number of males from the county in Australia.

On researching in County Archives or reading past editions of north Wales newspapers it is surprising to find how many sentences of transportation were passed by the courts. Speaking as one who has no convict connections, what is more surprising still is that the reluctance of surviving families to talk about past cases seems only slowly to be waning. Though a number of facts have been made known in conversations and correspondence, they were made with the caveat that present-day relatives are not to be mentioned in print. On the other hand, Australians from 'convict backgrounds' seem to pride themselves if they have such connections. Such stories would make wonderful films!

It has not been possible to include details of every case from the counties of Anglesey, Caernarvon, Merioneth, Denbigh and Flint in this book, as it would then become an encyclopaedia! Hopefully, readers will enhance their knowledge by further reading and study in local archives, and by bringing cases and stories to light amongst their own families and in their own areas.

Most of the cases highlighted had a detrimental effect and influence on relatively few lives outside immediate families and victims – not enough to make them cases of 'national' importance – but they have their part, and a significant one at that, in Welsh history, and in the legal and social history of Great Britain, America and Australia.

That is why none of them should ever be forgotten.

Chapter 1

Who were they, and what language did they speak?

A study of transportees' surnames shows that many had Welsh roots, as the names in question are found in any and all lists of Welsh surnames. 'Common or garden' Welsh surnames such as Jones and Hughes are abundant, as are others of an earlier derivation and ones from further afield.

The further west one goes in north Wales, the more Jones features in the list; followed fairly closely by Roberts and Williams. Other names recognised as being Welsh include Hughes; David/Davies; Owen/Owens; Thomas; Parry and Evans. These names are more abundant in the counties of Anglesey, Caernarvon and Merioneth, whilst the lists for the more easterly counties of Denbigh and Flint contain only a few Welsh names – but are full of non-Welsh-sounding ones such as Appleton; Burke; Doulben; Frumstone; Gratton; Hiles; Hodgson; Jervice; Kenison, etc. This is due to the closeness of the English border, and the free migration of families from Liverpool, Manchester, Cheshire and Lancashire to the more industrialised areas of north Wales.

Everyone has their own full name and title, but criminals and villains sometimes use an alias. A simple change of name might involve changing William to Billy, or a Robert known as Robin Hughes. Changing Evan Evans to Evan Jones might be enough for some, but for others only a complete change would suffice e.g. Thomas Evans was also known as John Parry. Why was John Davies also known as John Conway? Was he from the castle town? Might he even have been a sailor on the warship of

14

that name? John is too long gone by now for us to find out. Married women sometimes held on to their maiden names, so Jane Roberts was also known as Jane Williams – which might have confused the authorities. Other married women were known by their husband's name – Mary the wife of John.

Others had nicknames, e.g. Susan the Carrier. David Evan was known to his associates as Deio'r Oen (Deio the Lamb). Was he just a simple shepherd? Some had their trade added to their names, so James Williams was also known as James the Butcher. Thomas Roberts otherwise known as Tom Gors could have been suggesting where he lived. William Jones alias William Hardy alias Wil Mutton Hall appears to be a very descriptive alias.

For some, a description was added to their names on the documents, which helps the twenty-first century reader to build a profile of the individual in question – but which did the person no favours at the time. The writers or clerks of the courts did not beat about the bush:

'an idle person, a man of low stature and blind in one eye.'
'rather short according to his age, free of any marks of smallpox and his clothes are very old and ragged.'
'a woman of ill-fame – who used to wander about sleeping nights in hovels.'
'a common prostitute.'
'light characters'
'an old offender'
'a Baptist dairy maid in her 20s, a fresh faced girl with a ruddy complexion and freckles'
'a poor man from Anglesey' (weren't they all ?)
'a poor creature with white lips calling herself a domestic servant'
'a scally' – letting us, today, know straight away that his roots at least were on Merseyside;
'one of a notorious gang'
'cowardly, base assassins'

and finally a description that, had it been written today, would merit a law suit against the journalist who wrote it:

> Appearance of prisoner was truculant [*sic*]. A low receding forehead, from which deep set eyes, under shaggy eyebrows peered out at times around the court furtively and then dropped. A red beard grown full up and around the closely pursed lips which were kept constantly twitching and a prominent pock pitted nose completed the prisoner's forbidding facial aspect. He stood at the dock at once an object of pity and loathing.

To get as full a profile as possible of those who were transported, it helps to know their occupation. Many were labelled as 'labourers' – who no doubt worked for low wages and found it very difficult to make ends meet. Other known occupations are fairly common – for example, weaver, butcher, servant, soldier, mariner etc. Also included are vital jobs in an agricultural community e.g. blacksmith, sow gelder, skinner.

More specialised trades were room painter, cooper, shoe maker, gardener, buckle maker, hosier (in the stocking trade), tailor, mop maker and maltster. In a more industrialised area collier, reeve – a person in authority such as a steward or bailiff; corviser – a person carrying a corvier (a basket used for carrying minerals or ores in a mine) and even a huxter (one who goes about selling small items i.e. a pedlar) are listed. These were ordinary men and women who had to make a living.

Others were not employed and described as being married, unmarried, a spinster, single woman or widow. The 'unfortunates' who had no home were mere pedlars or tinkers but there were some who had fallen from grace i.e. gentleman and yeoman – who put themselves a step above ordinary folk and farmers. They had small estates to support themselves and families – but not enough land or capital for them to be called 'gentry'. In fact, they were 'gentlemen farmers' who, unfortunately for them, joined the long list of offenders.

The eighteenth and nineteenth centuries saw many marked changes in Wales and Welsh life in general, with a massive population increase due to immigration and to the fact that Wales was beginning to find her place in the British Empire. Industrialisation also forged many changes upon the country, which was until then looked down upon by its neighbour – England.

At that time, Wales was mainly an agricultural country, but a few heavy industries such as lead and iron provided resources for a general demand to supply Britain during a time of war against France and Spain. In Denbighshire, the Myddletons of Chirk, and in Flintshire Lord Grosvenor, were seen as the leading families to develop these heavy industries. Copper workings at Parys Mountain, Anglesey, flourished. The ironworks of Flint and east Denbigh were nurtured by John Wilkinson of Whitehaven, and as the surrounding countryside lacked food and a working population, many thousands moved in to take advantage of the opportunities offered them by the new industries. The slate quarries of Caernarvonshire and Merionethshire had huge supplies, which also necessitated a working population. Flintshire had a greater number of industries than any other north Wales county. Together with lead and coal mines, copper was mined in the county, cotton mills were built at Holywell and potteries were built at Buckley. All this industrialisation meant that, at times, there was industrial unrest. The working population had, many a time, to think hard where the next square meal was coming from. No wonder, therefore, that many turned to crime – not just because of their background (and some were, no doubt, habitual criminals) but because of other social needs and wants.

Today, different accents and dialects are heard daily with the BBC's so called 'estuary accent', broad Geordie and Cockney rhyming slang, and Prince Charles' 'cut glass' accent; many others are heard on various radio and TV programmes. Even so,

some of them can be quite difficult to follow and understand –
as it is in Wales, with a different version of Welsh spoken in
south Wales compared to what one hears in the north. One
wonders about the convicts who were transported to Australia
and whether they had any language difficulties. Did they
understand all the commands barked at them by figures in
authority? Were they able to follow instructions? Accents and
dialects heard in those days were confined to what could be
heard in the locality, but on finding themselves on board ship
bound for 'down under' they had to learn naval terms pretty
quickly in order to understand where to go and what to do.
Terms such as 'for'ard' and 'aft' would have meant very little to
most of them initially, and they probably didn't recognise
descriptions of themselves as 'snow gatherers' (ones who stole
clothing that had been left to dry and air on hedges), 'blue
hunters' (ones who stole lead from the roofs of buildings) or
'skinners' (ones who stole children or sailors' clothes) but they
may well have picked up some of the convicts' language during
their time in gaol, and other terms were learned when they
reached their destination (See Appendix 4).

But there must have been even worse language problems for
convicts who came from parts of Britain that had their own
language rather than English. Many of the Irish convicts were
Gaelic speakers and their lack of English 'contributed to a
damaging cocktail of misunderstanding and contempt.'
(Deborah Oxley.)

By 1852, about 1800 of the convicts had been sentenced in
Wales. Many who were sent there could only speak Welsh, so
as well as being exiled to a strange country they were unable
to speak with most of their fellow convicts.

(Martin Shipton, *Western Mail*, 2006)

Today, a few counties in Wales are considered more 'Welsh' than
others, but in the nineteenth century many parts of the country

had not been anglicised, and Welsh was the first language of many. A number of prisoners might have had no English at all. It may not be a surprise to note that one convict from Carmarthenshire never understood a word of what was said at her hearing, and an interpreter was asked to translate to her the sentence of the court. It may not be a surprise either that others from Anglesey, Caernarvonshire and Merionethshire were unable to follow the proceedings, but one, Elizabeth James, was from Cardiff, and even she had not mastered English, and was able to speak it only very badly.

It did not concern the ones who stood in judgment what levels of literacy and language skills those sentenced to be transported had, because once landed in Australia the King's/Queen's English was quickly learnt by all who had failed to keep the King's/Queen's Laws.

Lewis Lloyd, in *Australians from Wales* makes the point that a study of the first language of convicts from Wales has not been made and unfortunately such information is not now available. 'Of the British migrant population of Australia, only the Welsh have been almost entirely overlooked.' (Dr Arthur F. Hughes.) This is because there were comparatively few of them, and the use of the term 'England and Wales' in official records did not accurately state where convicts came from and dismissed the fact that some, at least, could speak Welsh. 'The history of Australia may be stated simply: the English made the laws, the Scots made the money, the Irish made the songs. The Welsh? They contributed very little ...' (E. Campion).

But that there were monoglot Welsh speakers amongst those who were convicted cannot be denied, and not all came from rural counties or communities. Life in Australia may well have been easier for native Irish and Scottish Gaelic speakers, as many more of their countrymen were sent out, and holding a conversation in their mother-tongue must have been easier. But for every 1,000 convicts on the transport ships there were only about fifteen from Wales. Confusion, loneliness and isolation must have been felt much more by such Welsh speakers. For those few Welsh-speakers who were sent out to Australia, going to chapel was one way of keeping their language alive, for even if they had to learn and speak English at work, many worshipped in their first language. This gave them a sense of still belonging to the 'mother country', and they held literary festivals and eisteddfodau. The first eisteddfod was held in Victoria in 1836.

When Kay Daniels wrote of Maria Lord, one who was transported to Van Diemen's Land and later became a noteworthy historical figure, she emphasized how few facts are known about Maria:

> What we know about Maria Lord is so little that it would be rash to call it a biography. There are no diaries or personal letters. No text reveals her inner life or her daily experiences. There is no portrait or sketch. What is known about the first twenty years of her life fills half a page, and little more is known about the last thirty.

This is true of many if not most of those transported from Britain. Anne Williams alias Edwards of Llanfechell, Anglesey was one. Few facts are known about her. She was, like many of her fellow travellers, described as a housemaid, kitchen servant, cook, farm servant or milking maid, who worked for a paltry wage of between four and six pence a day. But that, really, tells us very little, and we can only guess at her level of literacy. Was she bilingual? Could she read? Could she write?

The first school in Llanfechell was established by Richard Wynne in 1723, but there were only four boys on the register by 1831. The first Methodist Schoolroom was opened in the village in 1815 by Mr. John Elias, son of the Reverend John Elias. By 1823 the congregation grew strong enough to support a class or school, which met every Thursday night in a carpenter's workshop, and a morning Sunday school, which opened at 6 a.m.

Further developments saw the building of a schoolroom in 1832.

There was some opportunity to better oneself even in a relatively out of the way place such as Llanfechell, but most parents failed to recognise the importance of a sound education for their children, and many were sent out to work to support the family as soon as possible.

Inspector John James, whose report appeared in *The Reports of the Commissioners of Enquiry into the State of Education in Wales (1847)* (commonly known in Wales as 'The Blue Books Report') was highly critical of Llanfechell School. After praising the curriculum offered at the school, which included reading, writing, arithmetic, grammar, geography, seamanship, Religious Instruction and the Catechism, he criticized the achievements of the pupils who were in school on 12 November 1847:

> nine could read fairly . . . out of nine who were learning arithmetic, three could work sums in Proportion. Only one knew anything of Geography, and that was very little. There was no one who could repeat any of the Church Catechism owing to the objection of the parents. Three were able to answer Scripture questions well; others showed great ignorance of the subject. One said John the Baptist was the Son of God, and another that it was Adam and his family who went into the Ark. Thirty five scholars were above ten years of age. A few of the other children could understand a little English; but the majority were reading words which, to them had no meaning. The master speaks English fairly. He does not control the children; there was no discipline in his school . . .

These commissioners from England, none of whom spoke any Welsh, failed to understand that most of the children in the school were monoglot Welsh, who spoke nothing but Welsh at home. If they were being taught in English it is hardly surprising that they had learned little.

Did Anne take advantage of the educational opportunities Llanfechell had to offer? Had she been to school? Could she speak and understand English? All the answers to the above questions can only be guessed at, but an ability or lack of ability to read, speak and understand a second language must have played a big part in the formation of her character.

As with others who appeared in the same court as her, Anne was most probably almost a monoglot Welsh-speaker. However, all legal business at that time was conducted in English, making it very difficult for someone who was unfamiliar with the language on a day-to-day basis, let alone the legal jargon. Of the twenty-one gentlemen named on the jury for her case hearing in Beaumaris, it is doubtful if even half of them could speak Welsh.

Anne was sentenced to be transported and spent time in Millbank Prison in London. It is almost certain that the Anne Williams referred to in *Memorials of Millbank and Chapters in Prison History* (A. Griffiths, London 1884) is the same Anne Williams alias Edwards of Llanfechell, Anglesey:

> Repeated attempts at suicide, self mutilation and starvation, along with the use of 'dreadful' language, led Ann Williams' demeanour to be described as showing 'strongly of artifice' for which the doctor recommended punishment – a bread and water diet.

But was it 'dreadful language' or was she just speaking and/or swearing in Welsh? Those in London had very little knowledge of Welsh and probably did not recognise the language.

On board the transport ship *Garland Grove*, on which Anne travelled to Van Diemen's Land, a Miss Lang Grindod held school classes. All the women on board were pupils. Anne joined them. According to court documents in Beaumaris, she was 'illiterate' – that is, she could probably read and write in Welsh but possibly not in English. According to Miss Lang Grindod, her loneliness, due to her lack of English, was quite apparent to her fellow travellers and to her teacher, but sympathy was in very short supply:'Anne is dismissed in a single word – BAD'.

One fact that is apparent about convicts such as Anne, and others from Wales who had little English at the time of sentence, is that they must have been quick learners or they would have found it very difficult to survive in Van Diemen's Land. Most of them, to their credit, did so, and raised families, and one can only wonder whether they brought up their children to be bilingual – or was it easier to forget the old language and concentrate on their new life in a New World?

Chapter 2

America – Land of the Free?

Certain words or sayings have the power to frighten the listener and send shivers down their spine. 'Transportation' was one such word. How many criminals or 'victims', in a court of law, trembled at the knees when the judge pronounced a sentence of transportation 'to such place beyond the seas as her Majesty in Council might deem fit'?

When the term 'transportation' comes to mind, one tends to think of Australia – as 'Terra Australis' seems to be almost as far away 'beyond the seas' as one can go, or rather, be sent (apart from New Zealand). However, there were other horrors to which criminals could be sent. Africa and America were also used, and there were instances of places nearer to home being cited as eventual destinations. In his diary for 28 April 1742, William Bulkeley of Brynddu, Llanfechell, Anglesey relates how he and William Lewis of Llys Dulas, Anglesey sat listening to a case at the Quarter Sessions held in Beaumaris. Before the court were:

> two incorrigible rogues, Irish by birth, to be sent to the house of correction in Holyhead and to be kept there for a month at hard labour and every Saturday to be well whippt from Pepper Hall to the Cold Harbour, and afterwards to be transported to Ireland.

Could it be that they thought of getting an easy passage home? It seems their plan backfired – badly!

Transportation as a form of punishment probably dates back

to 1584 when Richard Hakluyt, a cleric, geographer and historian, thought it could be useful to send convicts to cut down trees and plant sugar cane in the newly discovered and developing colonies of America and the West Indies.

In 1597, during the reign of Queen Elizabeth I, a law – '39 Eliz.c.4 An Acte for Punyshment of Rogues, Vagabonds and Sturdy Beggars' was drafted which ordered such people to 'be banished out of this Realm . . . and shall be conveyed to such parts beyond the seas as shall be . . . assigned by the Privy Council.' Should any '. . . Rogue so banished . . .' have returned to England, without permission, they were to be hanged. The Privy Council, in 1615, ordered that anyone convicted of serious offences could be sent as forced labour to either the East Indies or North America.

In the seventeenth century, prisoners sentenced to death had their sentences commuted and sent to the Plantations of the Virginia Company owned by Sir Thomas Dale, marshall of Virginia, America. Three hundred 'disorderly persons' were sent there in 1611, but many proved to be so 'profane and mutinous . . . diseased and crazed that not sixty of them may be employed.' Nevertheless, such persons were deemed more suitable than local Indians, who could not be imprisoned and used as forced labour, and the New World gentry were not the type to dirty their hands with manual labour of any kind. Such was the need for labourers that Dale asked for another two thousand 'offenders out of the common gaols condemned to die' to be sent out to the provinces for at least three years. As the Spaniards had already peopled their provinces in such a way, why not the English?

From 1618 onwards, groups of 'felons' were regularly sent to the New England state of Massachusetts in the north, and to the southern parts of the New World. It is said that 1,500 children were sent out to Virginia in 1626. 'Nap' was an old word for stealing; 'kid' is slang for a child, so kidnapping meant taking children to work, as servants in America, by force. In 1650 and

1651, following the Battles of Dunbar and Worcester, Cromwell sent groups of prisoners of war and also a number of Irishmen who defied his attacks on Ireland to the West Indies. Acts of Parliament targeting law breakers, 'idle and wandering persons', Quakers, etc. were passed, detailing where such people could be sent. The Transportation Act of 1718 gave justices the right to sentence prisoners to seven years transportation if they claimed 'Benefit of Clergy', and up to fourteen years for a capital offence.

Another law was passed during George II's reign – George I, 4 Geo1,c.11 – which stated that anyone found guilty of a minor offence was to be transported to the Americas rather than be beaten or branded. Those in receipt of the King's Pardon following a capital offence were to be transported for fourteen years. During the next sixty years almost 40.000 – 30,000 British and 10,000 Irishmen – were transported. This, in turn, kept the English prison population down – but in 1775, following the American Revolution, British prisoners were refused as the number of imported black slaves increased to about forty-seven thousand a year. George III hoped that the political climate would change so that more prisoners could be sent across the Atlantic. 'Undoubtedly the Americans cannot expect nor ever will receive any favour from Me, but the permitting them to obtain Men unworthy to remain in this Island I shall certainly consent to.'

Transportation had to be stopped for the time being as the independent American colonies refused to acknowledge England's right to send any more convicts across the Atlantic. So worrying was the convicts' reputation that free settlers were deterred from going there. Something had to be done. For the time being all male convicts sentenced to transportation were kept at hard labour on prison hulks on the Thames, whilst women were kept in prisons.

During the seventeenth and eighteenth centuries some 50,000 convicts were transported, usually for seven years, to

America. Of that number the historian A. Roger Ekirch estimates that 36,000 came from England, 13,000 from Ireland and 700 from Scotland It is also known that the total figure includes some from Wales, including a few from Anglesey.

The arrival of convicts in America is described by Robert J. Brugger: 'Typically males of humble origins, the convicts arrived at either Annapolis or Baltimore chained in groups of ninety or more men, 'wretched, ragged and lean', as one of them recalled. Buyers came aboard, looked in mouths, and haggled over prices.'

Few Americans know anything about the 50,000 convicts transported there because the number of convicts was small compared to that of black slaves (about 721,000 in the 1790 census), and also because slavery was not abolished until 1863, whereas the flow of convicts ceased in 1776.

Mere statistics do not give a true representation – so who really were these people?

Margaret Stephen was a married woman from the parish of Llanidan. She has the doubtful honour of being the first from Anglesey to be transported anywhere in the world. It was her misfortune to be sent to America. Living close to the edge of the Menai Strait, it would have been convenient for her to cross over from her home to Caernarvonshire using either the Moel-y-Don or Tal-y-Foel ferry. For the journey to Caernarvon fair, the Tal-y-Foel ferry would have been best suited even though the ferryman would have had to skirt around a number of dangerous sandbanks.

It was to a Christmas fair held on a Saturday, 20 December 1730 that Margaret set off. Whilst moving from stall to stall, she stole a length of material together with two pewter plates belonging to John Parry of Ye Olde Bull's Head Inn, Beaumaris. Crowds of people would have made their way there on that day, and Margaret probably thought that she had a good chance of not being caught in the melée. Whatever her reasons for stealing, at the Court in Caernarvon on 24 November 1731 she was sentenced to be transported for seven years. What became of her is not known but she was the first to be transported from Anglesey.

The first male to be transported from Anglesey was John Probert Hughes, a labourer from Penrhoslligwy. His crime was breaking and entering a house and stealing clothing. His haul also included some silver buckles. He realized their worth and tried to fence them off to anyone who would pay a few pennies for them. Unfortunately, he chose the wrong person to deal with in John Williams, curate of St. Peter's church, Newborough, Anglesey who reported the crime to the authorities. John Probert was prosecuted by Owen Edward, Esquire. He was sentenced on 1 May 1734 to be transported for a term of seven years.

Maybe John Edwards of Mold, Flintshire, didn't realise what his haul included and that amongst the money he stole from Thomas Hewett on 10 January 1738 were gold moidores from Portugal. To John, they were most probably shiny objects worth more than what he could earn or had as savings. They certainly gave the game away when he tried to exchange them and he was sent to America as punishment.

It is understandable that someone is punished for stealing another's property, but in the case of unmarried Jane David of Holyhead one must sympathise a little with her because she was caught stealing clothing from her recently deceased father's house. Whatever her reasons for doing so, and the jury were not told, she was charged with stealing property worth 2/- from Anne Langford, a well-connected lady in town, whose connections with Jane's father were not explained, and was transported for seven years on 8 March 1740.

For some, crime may have been a way of life but for others it was a huge step down to find themselves in court. In the case of a stolen wig at Bangor on 16 October 1749, was it a clear cut case of theft or a misunderstanding between two gentlemen? A missing wig was reported to the authorities and an argument arose between two friends. One said it was his wig. The other said he had been given it. Whatever the truth, the argument became a fight about the ownership of a piece of horsehair. William Jones went home without a covering for his bald patch, but Richard Jones got off worse in the encounter: He was transported for seven years.

The charge sheet for William Jervice alias William Jervis of Ruabon, Denbighshire reads as follows:

13 September, 1750 – theft of gun locks, a fowling piece and a brass skillet belonging to the prosecutors Richard Jones, Edward Lloyd and Edward Williams.' Further details include the information that the 'prisoner had escaped from gaol' and that he had also been 'discharged for returning from transportation but detained for desertion.' He was transported for the second time for seven years.

Rowland Morris, by trade a 'sow gelder' from Llanllyfni, Arfon was punished by being transported for seven years for theft from a standing of shoes at Dinas Mawddwy fair in August 1752.

Mary Owen alias Mary Rowland alias Mary Morris, and Jane Tuson alias Jane Rowlands, both married women from Mallwyd, Merionethshire, were convicted of what in the twenty-first century would be called shoplifting, from the shop of Humphrey Roberts of Dolgellau - a mercer, i.e. a dealer in silks and velvets, on 2 March 1756. Their punishment was seven years transportation.

Around Christmas time 1756, Henry Williams alias Henry Roberts of Newmarket, Flint was found guilty of the theft of cloth belonging to John Jones, Elizabeth Williams, a widow and Thomas Edwards. 'The cloth was sold at Liverpool where the prisoner was apprehended'. He also, was transported for seven years.

Jane Edwards, a widow from Chirk, lived in a thatched

cottage. On 20 January 1757, Elizabeth Jones of Denbigh made a hole in the thatch, wriggled her way in and stole 'wearing apparel'. The value of the clothing was only 4d, but she was still transported to Australia.

The topic of conversation at the Tan y Bwlch Inn, Merionethshire on 11 May 1757 was the Corn Riots in Lleyn, and 'the mobs and how they proceeded'. Richard Francis knew quite well 'how they proceeded', as he was from Nefyn. He offered to sell the landlord a length of cloth that he was intending to sell in Montgomeryshire. How the authorities got to know about his whereabouts is not known, but he was caught. The owner of the cloth – Lowry Wynne, a widow from Edern, the parish next to Nefyn – pressed for a guilty verdict from the court and he was sent on his way to a the New World for seven years.

A month later, June 1757, Maurice Evan was sent to America as well. He was, firstly, sentenced to death, pardoned, then transported for seven years, and may well have set out on the same ship as Richard Francis. Maurice was a native of Llanddeiniolen, Caernarvonshire and regarded locally as 'a person of ill-fame.' He stole a sheep belonging to Jane Jones – the mother-in-law of William Griffith, who acted for the prosecution.

Most of the crimes which resulted in transportation to America and reported above involved the theft of either material or clothing, which shows the perpetrators as either being very poor and in great need or as persons with little regard for their fellow men. Obviously, in this period as in any other, there were such people who broke the law without much thought for their victims, but it is easy to believe that many were people in dire need.

It was about this time that another Anglesey man made his way to Virginia. Goronwy Owen, a renowned classic poet, set sail, with his family, from London to Virginia. He wrote to Richard Morris, his friend and mentor, from on board the Tryal at Spithead on 12 December 1757, 'we sail, as soon as the wind sets fair, with the rest of the convoy, which consists of about 300 other ships'. On board with Goronwy were about a hundred prisoners bound for the colonies. On arrival, they would be sold. A craftsman would fetch between £15 and £20, a labourer between £7 and £14, whilst women would be sold for between £7 and £10. Old and infirm prisoners would be sold for less. The working life of such ships would be between seven and fifteen years, as their condition would deteriorate rapidly in the north Atlantic Ocean.

William Dickenson's story sets the mind to wonder straight away as to why he was labelled a thief. His description reads: 'prisoner aged 16 years, rather short according to his age, free from any marks of smallpox and his clothes all very old and ragged.' He was also indicted for burglary as well as theft from John Read, a Hawarden collier, on 23 June, 1763. William, like John Edwards of Mold, a quarter of a century before, did not recognise the foreign coins included in his haul. His lack of knowledge of numismatology cost him his freedom for seven years.

A month later, William Roberts, who lodged in the house of Richard Jones (a Holywell baker), appeared before the same court on a charge of the theft of wearing apparel belonging to a fellow-lodger, Richard Williams (a Holywell labourer), the prosecutor. Williams always kept his better clothes locked up in a press, except when he wore them on Sundays or holidays. William Roberts had no holiday for the next seven years, as he was far away in America.

Many a small farmer has depended on help from a neighbour to bring in the harvest but David Morris of Llanrhaedr-ym-Mochnant had no such help. His neighbours waited until David and his family were out in the fields gathering the harvest at the height of Summer – 6 August 1767 – and then broke into David's house and stole personal goods and money. The thieves were Hugh Hughes and his brother (not named), from the nearby parish of Llanfwrog. Their sentence was one of seven years transportation.

Considering the poverty of the working class in the eighteenth century it is understandable why so many turned to stealing. Families had little to call their own. Wages were low and it was difficult to provide hearty meals for the table. That is probably why so many ventured out on dark nights to steal sheep. Mutton stew must have filled many a hungry belly. Was it for those reasons that John Roberts of Llanddyfnan near Llangefni stole one of his neighbour's sheep? Whatever the reason, Michael Hughes took him to court and on 3 November 1770 John was found guilty and punished by being transported for seven years.

Margaret Thomas of Llanbedrgoch, a rural Anglesey village was found guilty of stealing a cloak worth 8d and an apron worth 2d, the property of Lowry Jones who lived at Red Wharf Bay. The case was tried at the Quarter Sessions of 20 June 1773; Margaret was found guilty and sentenced to be transported for seven years. The same punishment was handed out to William Jones, a weaver from Holyhead, for stealing five shillings from the house of Judith David, a widow of the same town. He was found guilty on 20 April 1786. It is difficult to understand how they deserved the same sentence, as William stole six times what Margaret took. It is also difficult to understand why, as both prosecutor and defendant were from Anglesey, William was held in Caernarvon Gaol, and a 'bill of expenses re. food, clothing and irons was presented to the court in Beaumaris for a convict awaiting transportation in the custody of the gaoler of Caernarvon'.

Chapter 3

Did they find religion?

According to English law, 'Benefit of Clergy' was originally a means by which clergymen could claim that they were outside the jurisdiction of the civil courts and should be tried under canon or church law.

In time, persons pleading for this benefit were required to undertake a literacy test and had to read from the Bible. In 1351 Edward III changed the law and 'Benefit of Clergy' was officially open to all who could read. By tradition Psalm 51 – 'The Sinner's Psalm' – was used for the test:

Have mercy upon me, O God, according to thy loving kindness . . . Wash me thoroughly from mine iniquity, and cleanse me from my sin . . . For I acknowledge my transgressions: and my sin is ever before me . . . Behold, I was shapen in iniqujty; and in sin did my mother conceive me . . . Purge me with hyssop, and I shall be clean: wash me, and I shall be whiter than snow . . . Create in me a clean heart, O God; and renew a right spirit within me . . . Deliver me from bloodguiltiness, O God, thou God of my salvation: and my tongue shall sing aloud of thy righteousness.

It was known as the 'Neck Verse', because being able to recite it in court could save the prisoner's neck. Like any other system it was open to abuse, and as serious criminals appeared to be getting off lightly, changes had to be made. Henry VIII and Elizabeth I made many changes in the legislation.

Women were allowed to plead 'Benefit of Clergy' in 1624. In

1706, the reading test was abolished, and the right to appeal for the benefit was made available to all first-time offenders of lesser crimes. Under the 1718 Transportation Act, those who pleaded 'Benefit of Clergy' faced a sentence of up to seven years banishment or transportation to North America rather than a much more severe custodial sentence at home. The American Revolution in 1776 brought about the end of transportation to the colonies. Branding criminals was abolished in 1779 and 'Benefit of Clergy' was no longer an option in most cases. It was formally abolished by Parliament in 1827.

Many who stood before the courts of north Wales asked for 'Benefit of Clergy'. Whether their pleas had any influence on the judges is unknown but it may well have given them a measure of hope that they would be spared the ultimate sentence of death. David Griffith of Denbigh asked for 'Benefit of Clergy' in 1734 after he had been found guilty of burglary at a shop and warehouse and stealing money. He was transported for seven years.

Thomas Jones, a labourer from Holyhead, in 1735, travelled as far as Llanfrothen, Merionethshire where he stole clothing from the house of Edmwnd Pritchard, tailor. He appealed for the 'Benefit of Clergy' in court and his death sentence was commuted to one of transportation for seven years. In the same year, on 23 December 1735, Martha Owen of Corwen, Merionethshire who broke into her employer's house and stole clothing worth £2 3s. 6d. was another who pleaded for 'Benefit of Clergy' and was sentenced to be transported for seven years.

Elizabeth Luke of Penmon, worked as a maid for William Jones in Llanfaes, Anglesey. She was accused of stealing food and drink from her employer, and on pleading 'Benefit of Clergy' on 20 February 1741, was sentenced to be transported.

In Caernarvonshire court cases, pleas for 'Benefit' were heard from Owen Prichard of Penllech, accused of stealing clothing from his employer on 8 January 1742, and also from John William of Llanllechid who, on 13 September 1743, took a fancy to some 'wearing apparel' that he and his wife saw drying on a hedge. Both Owen and John were found guilty and transported for seven years. John Thomas, worked as a farm labourer for William Pritchard of Llangwyllog, Anglesey but was originally from Llandrillo-yn-Rhos, Denbighshire, and was caught in the act of stealing clothing from the house of Robert Ellis, his employer. He also pleaded 'Benefit of Clergy' but on 6 October 1743 was sentenced to be transported for seven years.

Circumstances forced some to break the Law. Such a man was Samuel Owens of Wrexham who was found guilty of theft of food, barley and corn from a boat. His crime was related to a Food Riot which occurred in Bangor-on-Dee in July 1789. He was another who was transported for seven years. Food riots again feature on the charge lists in 1796 when Anne Catherall and Elizabeth Huxley were both found guilty of stealing food at Hawarden, Flintshire.

A forty-three year old former soldier, Thomas Minshull, who had been whipped with a 'cat' (a 'cat o' nine tails' was a whip with nine ends with a hook on each) out of the army for being 'an incorrigible rogue' had stolen clothing and household goods with his wife from the house of John Evans of Hanmer, in Flintshire. They then pawned the clothing at a pawnbroker's shop in Chester and pocketed the money – £1 19s 6d – and for that he was transported for seven years. Rogue or not, he appealed for 'Benefit'.

Though this method of pleading for mercy was coming to an end, some made use of it in later years and appeared to have been successful in their pleading as they, like the others before them, were transported for only seven years when their crimes meant that could easily have been sentenced to much longer terms. The year 1817 must have been a trying one for judges and members of the jury as a number of offenders were tried and punished: Samuel Holland of Llangollen stole money in February; Elizabeth Emanuel, from Denbigh stole ribbons and shoe ornaments in June; in July Abel Hayes from Wrexham stole food and clothing including gaiters and stockings: Edward Jones and John Morris stole stockings from a carrier who had stopped overnight at Wrexham; William Davies and William Thomas stole poultry in October. All were transported for seven years.

Three other Denbighshire women pleaded for 'Benefit': Catherine Burke (alias Catherine Kay) in 1820, Anne Hiles in 1826 and Ellen Roberts also in 1826, but their appeals were unsuccessful as they were all transported for fourteen years each.

Others who were luckier were the ones who were sentenced to death but whose sentences were commuted and changed to one of transportation. Catherine Jones of Abererch was sentenced to death because she had broken into a dwelling house and stolen a newly-slaughtered calf. Her original intention was to steal potatoes, as she and her sister were very hungry. Elinor and John Samuel insisted on the ultimate penalty but had their wish turned down when Catherine was pardoned and transported for life.

Hunger may also have played a part in the robbery committed by David Jenkin of Tywyn, Merioneth. On 27 July 1754, he stole a bag, a handkerchief, a bag and mutton. This was classified as highway robbery for which the punishment was death. Luckily for him, he was pardoned and transported for fourteen years. Another highway robber was David Doulben, aged about twenty-two, of Llanynys, Denbigh. He was guilty of stealing money, sentenced to death, pardoned and also transported for fourteen years.

Stealing 'wearing apparel' was a fairly common crime, which gives an impression of how poor people were. John Davies of Hope broke into and entered a house and stole items of clothing. Originally sentenced to death, he was pardoned and transported for life.

Newspapers of the period were very willing to include the detail that prisoners had appealed for 'Benefit of Clergy' in their columns, but were reluctant to explain to their readers what exactly that meant and whether it had any bearing on the sentences passed.

Chapter 4

Prison hulks and convict ships

In 1776 a law – 16 Geo.III,c.43 'The Hulks Act' – was passed that decreed that old war, troop, convoy or merchant ships which were of no further use be situated in Plymouth, Portsmouth and Langston on the English south coast and also in Deptford and Woolwich, on the river Thames in London. Without masts or rigging, these would be suitable holding ships for prisoners. Those sentenced to transportation were also to be sent to the 'Hulk Ships' to await departure whilst the government of the day decided where exactly to send them to. During their imprisonment on the hulks, prisoners were expected to work for one of the local services. Up to 3,000 prisoners were held in what was an enclosed, self-sufficient community, each with its own hospital and under the supervision of inspectors and other officers, a chaplain and surgeon.

Life on board was hard for anyone who found themselves on the hulks. They would have, probably, suffered before their arrival as most had had a long journey in chains from court to the coast. So long, in fact, that some members of the public requested in the *Caernarvon Herald* on 1 November 1834 that a convict ship be anchored on the river Mersey to accommodate convicts from north Wales, Shropshire, Cheshire and Lancashire. This would reduce the expense of sending them to London or Portsmouth by at least a fifth.

Reducing the cost would have no effect on the prisoners as it was not a journey anyone could enjoy at the best of times, no matter how it was completed. Edward John Jones was originally convicted of stealing and killing a ewe worth 4/- in 1792; found guilty and sentenced to death which was commuted to one of transportation for seven years. Thomas Webster was guilty of Grand Larceny and also sentenced to be transported. Both were sent from Dolgellau Gaol on 23 November 1794 to Barmouth, where they boarded a sloop captained by Rees Griffith to embark on a sea voyage to London. The captain was paid £12 12s for his troubles.

Others from Meirioneth made the journey by road. Before starting from the gaol, they had to undergo a medical examination and if given a clean bill of health the certificate was given by the prison doctor to the escort. The prisoners were put in fetters – a job for which the local blacksmith was paid 2/-. The first leg, on horseback, was from Dolgellau to Shrewsbury with a breakfast stop at Dinas Mawddwy and a night's stop at Dolarddyn. A second stage was embarked on the following morning to reach Shrewsbury in time to catch the Mail Coach to London – tickets at 10/6 per passenger. On the route between Shrewsbury, Shifnal, Birmingham, St. Alban's and the Blossoms Inn, Lawrence, London – a grand hotel of twenty beds and stables – one escort stayed with the prisoner inside the coach but the assistant had to ride on top. It was another ten days before they could set sail, therefore another hotel was found before the escorts could return home. By now, the return tickets had risen in value to 16/- per passenger together with 8d. for stabling the horses in Shrewsbury, no wonder that a bill of £15 5s. was presented for a job that took from 5 to 24 February 1783.

Should any prisoner escape en route, the escort responsible for their transfer had to forfeit his payment for breaking his contract, and if no letter confirming safe arrival of the prisoner was produced, no costs were paid – as much as £34. 8s.2d for transferring two prisoners from Caernarvon to London in 1813.

After arriving at their destination, and registering, all were required to have a bath and change into the uniform of a rough, grey material. The experience of George Reading in 1841 was:

I was Striped of my Clous and then I was Put into a tub of water and wel washed allover and I neaver Saw my Clous after and then I Put on thear dress which was Course brown dress and then I had a hion Put round mileage and that was Fastned on my leage and I weared it day and night and it was Three Pounds and I wared it day and night.

The uniform served as their only set of clothes. Wages of a shilling per week were paid for any work completed, but the Government claimed most of it back. Prisoners were allowed one penny each; a third of which was retained and was returned as a lump sum towards the end of the sentence.

Life on the hulks was very difficult, especially so for young prisoners from a rural background and for those Welshmen who only spoke a few words of English. Facing the reality of not being able to see their families ever again, having to leave their homes and the land of their birth, must have been a very traumatic experience. Their daily life was regimented which, again, might well have been very different to the rural existence lived by many. Everyone was given 1¼ lbs. of bread, and a quart of gruel every morning and evening; on four weekdays they were allowed a piece of meat weighing no more than 14 oz. and on the other three days 4 oz. of cheese. Weak beer was served to everyone except those on hard labour, i.e. working on local highways or other Government sponsored work – who were allowed strong ale. Education for prisoners on board most of the hulks was non-existent. Knowing they were to be kept on board, in some cases for a number of years, must have been particularly heartbreaking as they were so near to home and yet so very far away.

In a report to one of the Government's committees in 1831, a full description of everyday life on the hulks was included. The report stresses that prisoners should be separated and that their punishment should be: 'sufficient to make it an object of terror to the evil doer'. But in reality, it was never thus and the whole system was found to be deficient, though the report did try to paper over some cracks:

> The ships are divided into wards, each containing from 12 to 30 persons; in these they are confined when not at labour in the dockyard, and the evil consequences of such associations may easily be conceived, even were the strictest discipline enforced.

The report complains that prisoners were allowed a light between decks until as late as 10 o'clock at night! Contrary to the regulations, dancing and singing were seen and heard. Disagreements and fights broke out regularly and the 'old lags' stole from the 'new hands' and, almost unbelievably, newspapers and books found their way on board! 'The indulgence of purchasing tea, bread, tobacco, &c. is allowed, the latter with a view to the health of the prisoners.'

Some family visits were arranged – but how could a family from Anglesey make its way down to London when such a journey for the prisoner and his or her guardian cost upwards of £14 (equivalent of £692.86 in 2010)! If a petition was sent by the family asking for a prisoner to be excused from hard labour, they were more often than not looked upon favourably. 'It is obvious that such communication must have the worst effect; it not only affords an indulgence to which no person in the situation of a convict is entitled, but it allows the most dangerous and improper intercourse to be kept up with his old companions, from whom it is most important to disconnect him.' With proper supervision, such a system could have been successful, especially if the on-board priest had been conscientious in his work all week long, but 'except for a short time on Sunday morning, the Chaplains have no communication whatever with them'.

It was also suggested that life on board the hulks was comparatively comfortable ('pretty jolly') and if prisoners could live with the shame of being there, they were, indeed much better off than most members of the working class of the time. 'Indeed, so far is this punishment from operating as a preventative to crime, that Your Committee have evidence that the situation of a convict has been regarded with envy by the free labourers who see him daily at his work; and the words of Mr. Lang, the master shipwright of Woolwich Dockyard, under whose superintendence all the convicts in that yard are placed, 'many labourers would be glad to change places with him, and would be much better off than they were before.'

Of the hulks used to hold north Wales convicts, the following can be seen as examples of how hard life was for those awaiting transportation:

Laurel – had been used for military prisoners before being referred to the prison service. In 1802, at Portsmouth harbour she was fitted out with separate ladders for each deck in preparation for housing 150 prisoners on her lower deck and another 121 in separate areas of the decks above. Convicts from the *Laurel* were in demand in the Portsmouth Dockyard and in Gosport as well, for they had a reputation of being hard workers. At Portsmouth Dockyard each man, whilst at work, was allowed an allowance of tuppence and a farthing per day and an additional halfpenny's worth of tobacco per day, for those who wanted it. If at Gosport, they received a pennyworth of biscuits, tobacco and beer each day. When released from Portsmouth, prisoners were given £1 16/-, and suitable clothing for a return to 'civvy street' was taken from the newly-admitted. There was no chapel on board but services were held on the spar deck with sailcloth canopies for protection against rain and bad weather. Mr. Donne, the chaplain, held services on alternate Sundays.

By 1815 the *Laurel* was at Gosport. She had been modified and refitted by convict labour. The refit meant there was room for fewer prisoners on board, which resulted in an improvement in safety arrangements.

Warrior – an ex navy, 74 gun, Man-O-War, built in 1781, with room for 600 prisoners. She was withdrawn from service in 1816 and moored on the Thames as a prison hulk in 1840 – after the American Revolution. In charge of her was John Capper, who for thirty years was Manager of The Hulk Establishment. In 1847, she was moved alongside the quay at Woolwich Dockyard and moored there so gas lighting could be installed. It was the only hulk to be so modified and was nicknamed 'the Model Hulk'. Even though gas lighting was an useful addition, the general condition of the ship was far from favourable. The governor's report stated that: 'It is well known that the hulk is in a most dilapidated condition, and scarcely able to hold together. Recent repairs supporting the lower deck & co have rendered her safe from any immediate danger; but the remedy is merely temporary. She is rotten and unsound from stem to stern.'

When prisoners were sent to the *Warrior* they were given a number which would have been printed on the back of their brown and red hooped uniform. Living accommodation was on three decks, with room for up to 200 convicts on each one. Each deck was divided into wards or cells, on either side of the hull, with a passage running down the centre. Each ward had two messes for eight to ten men, and in each a table and two benches. Fresh air was through the gun ports. There were small workshops for shoemaking and tailoring, which was done by convicts with those skills. A large chapel took up a sizeable part of the top and middle decks. There was a surgery, and a schoolroom. In each ward was a small library and every prisoner was issued with a library book, a Bible, a prayer book and a hymn book. In winter, fireplaces were lit in the passageways on every deck, and in the hold.

The working day began at 5.30 a.m. and everyone had 30 minutes to get dressed, washed, roll up and store their hammocks. Breakfast, which was served on wooden tables, consisted of 12 ounces of dry bread and a pint of cocoa per man.

At 7.15 a.m., after washing up, everyone was ready for the day's labours. Some stayed on board ship to clean, wash, cook etc. whilst the others were escorted to the dockyard by a military guard. Prisoners were guarded all day by soldiers with loaded weapons and fixed bayonets. In summer, it was a ten hour working day and 8½ hours in winter. The mid-day meal was eaten on board the hulk and was made up of 6 oz of meat, 1lbs potatoes and 9 oz of bread. Soup was also served on three weekdays.

At the end of the day, an hour and a quarter was allowed for washing, preparing, eating and cleaning up after a meal of a pint of gruel and 6 oz of bread. A further 2 hours were spent at prayer, school work, and repairing clothing. Hammocks were opened out at 9 p.m. in summer, or 8 p.m. in winter. The only changes to this regime came when all those on hard labour were required to spend one day out of every nine or ten days in the schoolroom.

A mutiny broke out on *Warrior* a few days before Christmas 1851. Prisoners took control of the under-decks and held the ship to ransom until Royal Marines were called to settle matters after which the leading prisoners were sent to Millbank Prison.

Capper became bored and ineffective in his work and 'allowed conditions to deteriorate'. *Warrior* continued in service until 1856 but was sold off soon after.

Using prison hulks was deemed a failure and by 1790 the number of prisoners was increasing at the rate of 1000 per year. 'Health and Safety' were issues to consider. The spread of typhus and other sickness worried the local population and the condition of the hulks deteriorated which only added to the problem.

When it was decided to use Australia as a destination for convicts, new ships were needed to transport them. 'The transports which conveyed the convicts to the Australian colonies were ordinary British merchantmen, such as might be seen the world over.' What became known as the 'First Fleet' set sail for Terra Australis. With their holds full to overflowing, eleven ships were prepared to begin their voyage from Portsmouth. They caught the 3 o'clock tide on the morning of 13 May 1787. The fleet was led by *Sirius* and the other naval ships which included the sloop *Supply*, and store ships – *Borrowdale* (272 tons), *Fishburn* (378 tons), and the *Golden Grove* (331 tons).

Prison ships included *Alexander* (452 tons), *Charlotte* (345 tons), *Friendship* (278 tons), *Lady Penrhyn* (338 tons) with a cargo of female prisoners, *Prince of Wales* (333 tons) with a cargo of mainly male prisoners, and the *Scarborough* (418 tons) built in 1781 and the oldest ship of the fleet.

The cost of hiring each vessel was 10/- per ton per month (nearly £20,000 then – £1,120,600.00 in 2010). Ridding the country of so many criminals proved a costly business.

Welsh prisoners amongst those travelling on the 'First Fleet' were:

- William Smith, sentenced at Denbigh.
- William Davies of Brecon – aged twenty-one, was tried on 12 July 1785. Sentenced to be transported for life, he set sail on the *Alexander*. During his period in Australia, he received twenty-five lashes from the cat-o'-nine-tails for setting fire to his hut, but it is not known if this was a deliberate act of arson or an accident, as his occupation was a baker. He died in 1830.
- Mary Watkins, nineteen years old from St.Andrew's, Glamorganshire – on the *Friendship*. She was tried at Cowbridge, Glamorgan on 25 April 1786 for robbery of 1 shilling and sentenced to transportation for seven years.
- Frances Williams of the parish of Whitford, Flint: a spinster who was prosecuted for burglary at the house of Moses Griffith, a painter from the same parish. She was also accused of stealing clothing and cloth worth £1 17s 5d. On making her escape, possibly to Liverpool, she was

apprehended by the ferry at Parkgate, Cheshire. Her plea of not guilty fell on deaf ears and so, on 1 August 1783 she was found guilty and sentenced to death, but she was pardoned and further sentenced to seven years transportation by the court in Mold, north Wales; she sailed on the *Prince of Wales*. Later she lent clothes to Elizabeth Pulley for her wedding to Anthony Rope – a marriage, in name at least, made in heaven!

- William Edmunds from Monmouth and tried at the same town on 21 March 1785 for stealing a heifer worth 80/-. His sentence of death was commuted to one of transportation for seven years. He set sail on the *Alexander*. At the time he was twenty-nine years of age and died 1843.

As well as those from Wales, about 730 other prisoners (560 males and 160 females) were forced on this epic voyage. Some of them were:

- Dorothy Handland (rag and bone dealer), eighty-eight years old in 1787 – the oldest transportee, sentenced for lying under oath. She also committed the first suicide in Australia in 1789.
- Joseph Owen, from Shropshire – the oldest male convict, though his age at the time was uncertain, but believed to be about sixty-six.
- John Hudson, the youngest child on board at nine years of age, sentenced to be transported for stealing a pistol and articles of clothing. A chimneysweep by trade, he did not get an opportunity to practise his craft in Australia, because when he arrived there were no houses, and those that were built soon after were very flimsy shacks without stone walls and chimneys.
- Elizabeth Hayward, a thirteen years old clog maker caught stealing a linen dress and a silk bonnet worth 7/-.

The 'Second Fleet' consisted of the *Guardian*, a 44-gun frigate (she was wrecked on False Beach, west Africa on 12 April 1790; twenty of her prisoners reached New South Wales and fourteen were given a conditional pardon for good conduct); *Justinian; Lady Juliana; Surprise; Neptune; Scarborough*. The *Lady Juliana*, which had left England in July 1789, arrived three weeks before the 'Second Fleet' with supplies and saved the occupants of the new settlement from starvation.

After voyages averaging 171.5 days the 'Third Fleet' arrived at Port Jackson during August, September and October 1791 to disembark their cargoes. From then on, until 1868 regular passages were made from England to supply the penal colonies. Many ships made the voyage back and forth from England to Australia; some more than once, e.g. the *Britannia*, but from 1821 onwards it became much more difficult to hire ships due to the ever-increasing need to convey free settlers to America and Australia in the search for gold. That took priority, and prisoners had to make do with whatever was available. In researching the history of convict ships it can be seen that some voyages became eventful ones, e.g. a mutiny on the *Marquis Cornwallis*; prisoner abuse on the *Britannia* and the mutiny leaders sentenced to be whipped three hundred times in one day and five hundred times on the second day of their punishment! Many lives were lost due to illness and disease, e.g. on the *Hillsborough* and the *Royal Admiral*.

Some voyages were completed in a relatively short time; others took much longer and some were never completed. The *Tellincherry, Neva, George III* and the *Boyd* were wrecked before arriving in Van Diemen's Land. The Emu was hijacked on 30 November 1812 by the American ship, *Holkar*, from New York. The crew and cargo of the *Barring* suffered from scurvy; the *Brothers* surgeon was attacked, and the *John* deliberately set on fire.

Eight hundred and twenty-five ships were used to convey prisoners from England to Australia – each showing a red and white pennant as a sign that they carried, on average, 200 prisoners. By 1800, and because of the Napoleonic Wars against France, only forty-two ships made the voyage. Between 1801 and 1813 no more than five ships per year arrived to anchor in Sydney. Up to 1814, 1,000 prisoners per year had arrived, but from 1815 onwards the floodgates were opened wide. Numbers reached a peak between 1831 and 1835 when 133 ships arrived with 27,731 prisoners on board. In 1833, thirty-six ships carried 6,709 prisoners to Australia, leaving 4,000 in New South Wales and the others in Van Diemen's Land. It was a long and hard voyage for all involved, with the First Fleet taking 252 days to reach their destination. By 1830, the time had been halved and the voyage completed in 110 days. Some, such as the *Eliza I* in 1820, the *Guildford* in 1822, and the *Norfolk* in 1829 took less than that, and the fastest voyage of all was made by the *Emma Eugenia* in ninety-five days in 1838.

Camden, Calvert & King were the company mostly responsible for the supply of ships, food and clothing for prisoners for the first three fleets, but due to carelessness on their part and prisoners arriving in a very poor condition, they were relieved of their duties and lost the contract.

From 1801 onwards, convict ships were sent out twice yearly – at the end of May and the beginning of September – to avoid the harsh winter and storms of the Southern Ocean. The last prisoner-carrying ship was the *Hougoumont*, which sailed in 1867 with, amongst others, a cargo of Irish Fenian prisoners (Fenians = Catholic nationalists from Ulster) on board to Western Australia.

Amongst other ships which transported prisoners from north Wales were (see also Appendix 2):

Earl of Liverpool: as well as convicts, there were a further eighty-two passengers on board, sixty-eight of which were pensioner guards (retired soldiers who had volunteered as guards on convict ships and after their arrival, were granted 10 acres of land and help in building a cottage) and their families. The group consisted of thirty guards, sixteen wives, ten sons and twelve daughters. The other fourteen travellers were either soldiers or cabin passengers. The *Earl of Liverpool* was, at the time, the ninth oldest ship afloat in the World; the oldest wooden merchant ship afloat; the last surviving Crimea War troopship; the last surviving convict ship to Australia and the last surviving wooden immigrant ship to New Zealand.

Garland Grove: on the 1842/43 voyage, the Second Officer, Abraham Harvey, kept a diary. He joined the ship in August 1842 whilst she was being fitted out at Deptford. He described the accommodation for the convicts as: '. . . similar to our emigrant ship, having two tiers of sleeping berths on each side, four abreast, each person with the addition of substantial triangular stanchions. provided with separate bed and bedding around the hatchways from the lower to the upper decks. Communications being left in the main and after hatchways through two small doors which were locked every night at 6 o'clock. To have the ship thoroughly ventilated being fitted with patent side scuttles and deck ventilator which were open during the day and secured at night. Also provided in the wind sails for the hatchway and provided with hanging stoves to burn coke to dry between decks. Commodious hospital fitted at the stern of the ship in which the main and after hatchway lights were kept burning during the night.'

In his reminiscences, Harvey goes on to describe how the convicts on board were visited by 'those truly heroic and self denying ladies that formed the Committee for visiting the Metropolitan Prisons . . . and occasionally accompanied by a Minister of the Gospel'. He further describes the scene when parents were able to visit their daughters on board and when it came to leaving time he 'witnessed many a heart-rending scene. Poor old men and women, some of them coming many miles to take a last Farwell of their erring daughters and in most cases, never more to see them again on earth'. The ship 'took our departure of the land of Old England' on 4 October. By 27 October the first funeral had been conducted by the Commander and Harvey himself officiated as Clerk. When 'the body was launched into the deep, a universal shudder came over all present'. On 18 January 1843, in the evening, they sighted the South Western parts of Van Diemen's Land. By the 20th, the ship took a pilot for Hobart Town and 'the women cheering most lustily at the thought of being so near the end of their journey. 9 pm, anchored at Hobart Town.' In May 1851, the *Garland Grove* was wrecked on rocks near Mauritius. Her crew and a cargo of mail were rescued.

George III: after leaving the Downs, an outbreak of scurvy hit the ship due to poor quality food and the fact that coffee was used instead of oatmeal in the prisoners diet!

On 27 January 1835, six weeks out of London and almost on the Line (Equator) the ship caught fire! Two prisoners grabbed hold of two barrels of gunpowder and carried them clear of the fire. Though their efforts certainly deserved some form of recompense, the captain refused to call at either Rio de Janeiro or the Cape of Good Hope, so everyone suffered because of the lack of supplies on board. By 12 April 1835 twelve prisoners had died; another sixty were on the sick list – fifty of whom were confined to bed and were utterly helpless.

Land was sighted at Port Davey; the sea was calm; weather mild; visibility good but at 9.30 p.m., the ship struck an unknown rock (now known as King George Rock). When the waves broke over the ship the mainmast broke. The third mate, thinking he was much nearer Hobart than he actually was, took two days to reach safety and seek assistance. Two paddle steamers were sent to assist. Of the 294 on board, 161 were saved; 133 (convicts) drowned. Credit was given at an inquiry into the tragedy to Moxey for his work in attempting to rescue as many as he could (though no real attempt was made to rescue the convicts) and as the rock was unknown, he was cleared of any blame for the loss of his ship, which on the inquiry deemed to have been unavoidable.

John Barry: this was a ship with a reputation for brutal treatment of those on board. During a 1819 voyage, one man was whipped seventy-two times; another received forty lashes. A mutiny, of sorts, was squashed on board ship on 18 August 1821. At 7.30 p.m., whilst the ship was at Lat. 22° 47′ S, Long. 40° 55′ W, three musket shots were heard. Before the crew were able to reach the confined spaces below decks, further shots were fired and three prisoners wounded. Surgeon Daniel McNamara handcuffed five ringleaders. Reports suggest that the trouble started when a nervous sentry, who was worse for wear with drink, fired to quieten threatening and noisy convicts. Conflicting reports were presented by the sentry and convicts but though the sentry was arrested, no details of what punishment was meted out to him survive.

Nile: one of the first ships to be issued with special instructions by Transport Commissioners for the voyage to Australia. They stressed the need for cleanliness, proper ventilation; that sleeping quarters were to be swept and cleaned daily, every fortnight bottom boards of beds were to be washed with sea-water and dried before being replaced, all bedding to be aired daily on deck; air scuttles were to be kept open; the sick were to be allowed free access to the deck, all illness to be reported and medicine used to relieve sickness; the hospital was to be kept clean at all times; all prisoners to be allowed two daily visits to the upper deck; lemon juice, sugar, sago, rice, oatmeal, peas, bread, wine and tea were to be used to stop any outbreak of scurvy.

The remaining ships are from a list of a total of forty-three ships (see Appendix 2) that transported convicts to Western Australia:
Hougoumont: a four-masted, 875 ton frigate, length 167 feet, breadth 34 feet. Launched in Boulmein, Burma and named after one of the farms on the site of the Battle of Waterloo.
Lord Raglan: the two reported deaths from amongst the convicts on board were James Railton and Emanuel Hatchard. Of the 270

convicts, 238 could read and write; 20 could read only and 12 could neither read nor write. Of the other 84 passengers, 30 were pensioner guards (including 1 sergeant major, 1 sergeant, 2 corporals, 26 privates), 21 wives, 11 sons and 18 daughters. The other four travellers were probably warders. One of the convicts – Stephen Stout, who in the surgeon's opinion could be considered 'a good scholar' edited a newspaper titled *Life Boat* during the voyage. He also delivered lectures on such diverse topics as 'Eclipses' with special reference to an eclipse of the sun, and also on 'Australia' and 'Australian Employment.'

Western Australia, 1842 miles (and today, two time zones) away from the east coast penal settlements, became a free colony in 1829. It was not until 1850, however, that convicts were accepted. It is said that the need for cheap labour for the settlers already there was the main reason why the state changed its status from 'free' to 'penal'. Britain was still in need of somewhere to off-load convicts and the eastern states of Australia were, by then, closing down their prisons and penal settlements. If sent to Western Australia, the 9,270 convicts could have been sentenced to six, seven, ten, fourteen, or fifteen year terms. It is also noted that many of them were more experienced law-breakers and their crimes far more serious. They were also found to be much more literate. When their term of transportation came to an end, about one third of them left the area. Whatever happened to them, they also have their part to play in the history of Australia.

Chapter 5

Living 'tax-free' in Botany Bay!

They go off an island to take special charge,
Warmer than Britain and ten times as large,
No Customs House duty, no freightage to pay,
And tax free they live when at Botany Bay.

(1786 ballad)

Transportation resumed in 1787 with a new destination: Australia. This was seen as a more serious punishment than imprisonment, since it involved exile to a distant land, with little, if any, chance of returning home when the sentence was completed. In the early nineteenth century, as part of the revisions of the criminal law, transportation for life was substituted as the maximum punishment for several offences which had previously been punishable by death.

In 1779, a committee was convened by the House of Commons to further discuss the matter of convicts sentenced to be transported overseas, and where exactly they should be sent if the American colonies were unwilling to accept them. Wherever it would be, it would have to be far from Britain but able to sustain a settlement and population of its own – even though they would mostly be convicts and lawbreakers. Joseph Banks was asked for his views on the subject and he praised Botany Bay as a suitable site. Others did the same for Gibraltar and the western coast of Africa but the committee could not come to a decision and the matter was left undecided for the time being.

Jeremy Bentham, reformer and a firm critic of transportation, spoke against the choice of Australia:

I sentence you, but to what I know not; perhaps to storm and shipwreck, perhaps to infectious disorders, perhaps to famine, perhaps to be massacred by savages, perhaps to be devoured by wild beasts. Anyway – take your chance; perish or prosper, suffer or enjoy; I rid myself of the sight of you.

When convicts were transported to America, there was a 'middleman' there to meet, buy and sell and set them all to work. This, in reality, meant little, if any, responsibility fell on the British Government's shoulders once they had left these shores. But sending them to Australia was a different matter altogether. Ships had to be sent out with their human cargoes but would have to return empty! There would be no reception committee to greet the new arrivals. No organised work would await them. Someone would have to finance such a scheme. The government, under William Pitt the Younger, was almost bankrupt. The sum of £29,000 needed to set up a penal colony and another £41,000 to maintain the settlement until it became self-sufficient was more than they could afford. On the other hand, the government could not allow France and Holland the upper hand in the Far East. India was also a gem to be guarded at all costs. A British presence had to be maintained, and it was for these reasons, mainly, that after lengthy discussion Botany Bay was chosen as the ideal site for transportation.

Pine and flax were of paramount importance to the ships of the Royal Navy in the eighteenth century. Masts were made of pine and for a seventy-four gun warship the main mast had to be three feet in diameter at the bottom, rising to a height of one hundred and eight feet. The timber had to be in perfect condition, without flaw. For the same ship a total of twenty-two masts were needed altogether, and hundreds of square yards of flax for the sails. In 1780, these commodities were mainly to be had in Russia, but the voyage there and back could often be troublesome. When the arrangements were put at risk, an alternative had to be found. In his reports about the 'Southern Continent', Joseph

Banks mentioned Norfolk Island, a thousand miles north of Botany Bay and discovered by Cook in 1774. It was also described as, more or less, the ideal place for a plentiful supply of pine and flax. There was no better site for the Royal Navy to establish a base and make use of the land of nearby Australia as a penal colony to dump an unwanted portion of the population

Even so, Pitt was not persuaded. Discussions continued and James Mario Matra, an ex *Endeavour* (Captain Cook's ship) officer, was called upon to try and persuade Lord North to use New South Wales as the place for settlers. No mention of a penal colony was made at this time. When the Earl of Sydney was appointed Home and Foreign Secretary in 1783, his main problem was still prison hulks and what to do about the prisoners. Matra resurrected his idea once more – only this time he included a solution to Earl Sydney's problem as well. 'Give them a few acres of ground as they arrive ... with what assistance they may want to till them. Let it be here remarked that they can not fly from the country, that they have no temptation to theft, and that they must work or starve.'

Other ideas and suggestions were put forward but no decision arrived at. On 20 April 1785 another committee under the chairmanship of Lord Beauchamp met to resolve, once and for all, this ever-increasing problem. Lemane Island, on the banks of the river Gambia in west Africa, was suggested. So were Das Volta Bay in the Orange river estuary, south west Africa, and Botany Bay, again.

In 1786, the decision was taken to use Botany Bay, it being the ideal place in the committee's eye, and with their decision a note was included to remind everyone of the purpose of the site chosen:

His Majesty's Colony of Van Diemen's Land is not intended to reform criminals, but simply to store them, like so much rubbish in a dust heap, so that England can be emptied of trouble makers once and for all.

A plan was formulated and presented to the Cabinet in August of the same year to send out up to six hundred prisoners on the First Fleet. Captain Arthur Philip, 'a remarkably humane man for such a brutish enterprise' was invited by George III on 12 October 1786 to take responsibility for the voyage and of the penal colony on arrival.

On arrival, prisoners were set to work in the Government's name and, after a probationary period, were assigned to free settlers to work on the land as bonded slaves. In time, and with a good reputation for hard work, they were allowed a 'Ticket of Leave'. A Ticket of Leave was issued to convicts who had served a period of probation, and who had shown by their good behaviour that they could be trusted. Once granted a Ticket of Leave, a convict could look for employment within a specified area but could not leave that area without permission. Ticket of Leave men could marry or bring their families from Britain (if they could afford to pay for their passage) and acquire property, but they were not permitted to board a ship or carry firearms. They were often required to repay the cost of their passage to Australia. The ticket had to be renewed annually and if not done could be lost for the slightest of reasons, e.g. laziness, being cheeky, showing disrespect to an officer, soldier or constable, or even for charging too high a price for any work done outside official working hours. Holders had to attend muster and church services. A convict who kept to the conditions of his Ticket of Leave until half of his sentence was completed was entitled to a Conditional Pardon, which gave the prisoner the right of state citizenship and removed all restrictions *except* the right to leave the colony. An Unconditional Pardon, which gave the prisoner the right to return home, was not often granted, except in exceptional circumstances.

Amongst the first from North Wales to be transported to Australia were:
• John Jones: He was a saddler from Amlwch, Anglesey who

obtained money by deception. His crime was presenting a bill to the Parys Mine Company for animal skins worth £12 12s. 6d. The prosecutor was William Hughes of Madyn Dusw. John appeared in court on 6 August 1787 and was sentenced to be transported for seven years. He had to wait four years before setting sail on the *Britannia* and he may well have been the '------ Jones, Anglesea' noted as being on the 'Third Fleet'.

- Thomas Jones of Llandderfel, Merionethshire, a labourer who was found guilty of stealing farm implements from Rev. Thomas Davies. The honourable gentleman did not forgive Thomas his trespasses, so despite his not guilty plea he was transported for seven years.
- William Smith alias William White, originally from Llandegla, Denbighshire, served as a soldier in the 40th Regiment of Foot, based at Chester. William was enjoying some home leave at his local inn with publican Thomas Roberts of Llandegla when he spotted a silver pint cup. He stole it, and for his crime was sentenced to a seven-year sentence of transportation on 14 August 1787.
- William Hughes, a mariner of no fixed address, was caught breaking and entering the house of Robert Hughes of Holywell and stealing 'wearing apparel', keys, a nutcracker and a 'steelyard'. On 24 September 1788 he was sentenced to be transported for seven years.
- John Royle of Mold was caught stealing the cattle of William Evans and Samuel Johnson on 13 February 1794. He was sentenced to death, but pardoned and transported for seven years.

On being sent to prison, one would expect to be faced with stone walls and iron bars but 'stone walls do not a prison make, Nor iron bars a cage . . .' (Richard Loveace 1618–1658). That was certainly true as regards Australia, for when the First Fleet arrived in 1788, there were no prisons there. In fact, there was hardly anything recognisable to those transported because nothing had been provided or prepared beforehand. Australia itself became, for a while, their prison. There was no means of escape. Even so, hundreds tried. Most failed.

When the convicts of the First Fleet disembarked, their transfer had to be completed. This involved the necessary and detailed paperwork which included all their details, e.g. place of birth, age, religion, physical description. The males were set to work almost immediately to build huts and shelters, but the females were kept on board ship for almost another week until roofs to put over their heads were ready. When it had been finished, Hyde Park Barracks was used as a place to wait assignment.

During the early days, female convicts lived the same life style as the males but supposedly in separate living accommodation – barracks and tents. In reality, after their long hours of labour – farming, cleaning, washing, or even rock-breaking for road-building – they returned to quarters which had been 'earned' by selling their bodies in return for shelter.

Elizabeth Fry spoke about conditions for women 'without shelter, without resource and without protection . . . a place to sleep in or the means to obtain one are, they were absolutely without . . .' Conditions for males were only slightly better. When public buildings had been built, forests cleared, roads through the bush laid, there was still a great deal to be done. Farming provided one answer and many were assigned to work the land of New South Wales and Victoria. Others were sent to places such as Moreton Bay, Port Maquarie, Newcastle or Norfolk Island. After 1850, the Swan River Colony was set up in Western Australia and Rottnest Island used as a prison. These settlements were built with punishment in mind and even today are still remembered for their brutal regimes. Another penal settlement was Maquarie Harbour, Van Diemen's Land – for re-offenders from New South Wales. When it closed, Port Arthur was opened – both institutions taking their names from governor generals – Lachlan Macquarie and Arthur Phillip.

Port Arthur began life as a timber station in 1830. Originally designed as a replacement for another closed timber camp at Birches Bay, Port Arthur grew in importance within the penal system. It was a penal station built in the bush, and other manufacturing businesses grew alongside such as shipbuilding, shoemaking, timber and brickmaking. By 1842 a flour mill and granary was being built, together with a hospital. In 1848 the first stone of a Separate Prison was laid. The Port was certainly a harsh place of punishment, for those in their cells could hear no sound: the guards wore slippers and carpets were laid down to deaden the noise. When they were allowed out of their cells, masks had to be worn so they could not recognise one another, and any conversation was soon stopped. By 1853 fewer transportees were arriving at the station, but Port Arthur was an important secondary punishment station. The last convict was shipped out in 1877. The site was renamed Carnarvon. Huge fires in 1895 and 1897 destroyed many old buildings, the prison and hospital but a new township arose from the ashes. In 1927 the name Port Arthur was reinstated.

Newcastle, situated 98 miles north of Sydney, was the first secondary penal colony established in Australia in 1804.

Port Macquarie was half way between Sydney and Brisbane.

Moreton Bay in south-east Queensland was originally home to Aboriginal tribes but in 1824 became a penal settlement for Sydney's worst offenders. The ballad *Moreton Bay*, which may be from around 1830, tells of life there, where 'Excessive tyranny each day prevails' under the Commandant, Patrick Logan. Between February and October 1928, Logan ordered 200 floggings. He was killed by Aborigines in 1830, and when his body was returned to the Bay the convicts rejoiced loudly all night.

Norfolk Island was settled in 1788; closed in 1814; re-opened in 1824. It was renowned for its harsh regime and fifty floggings per session was a common occurrence. Some convicts chose to be hanged rather than be sent there; others chose suicide on the way, which says a great deal about the severity of the treatment received out there. No wonder it was considered a living hell.

Maquarie Harbour, Tasmania – the actual prison was on Sarah Island in the middle of the harbour and was considered by the authorities to be escape-proof. This was why prisoners who had escaped from other prisons were sent there. All the convicts were involved in cutting down pine trees; building rafts so the logs could be sent down river. They had to work for up to twelve hours per day, wearing leg irons, in freezing cold water.

By 1804, female factories were opened. Here women lived and worked – sewing, spinning or working outside. They were also used as nurseries where convict women were allowed to keep their children for up to two years. Older children were allowed to stay only if the mother could prove that she could pay for their keep. Otherwise, they were sent to an orphanage. Women were classified into one of three different categories: a) the ones that no-one wanted to employ, b) those that had been returned to the authorities because they were unmanageable and to be punished further, c) pregnant women.

The first female factory was the one opened in *Parramatta*, New South Wales, in 1796. It was only a simple log-walled and thatched building used to hold re-offenders. When it burnt down, it was replaced with a two-storey stone building in 1802. This was also destroyed in a fire and a third building was built in 1804. The upper floor was called 'The Factory above the Gaol' and was used as a prison for juveniles and a workplace for female convicts. Had any female convict not been 'assigned' (hired out to work), she would find herself in the Female Factory. So many were sent there that the building was hopelessly inadequate. A new one, to hold 300 women, was designed by Francis Greenway and built in 1827 at a cost of £4,778 (worth £236,463.22 in 2010). Convict labour quarried the local sandstone from the other side of the Parramatta River to build a structure with walls 2' 6' thick for the ground floor and

1′ 8′ at the top of the third storey. It had oak shingles on the roof, barred windows in the basement, and lead-glazed lights on the other floors. The top two floors were sleeping accommodation whilst the first floor was for meals. By 1842, there were 1,203 women in the factory and when transportation ceased, it was converted to a Convict Lunatic Asylum in 1847. Today it houses a hospital and the New South Wales Institute of Forensic Psychiatry.

Other factories were opened at:

Cascades, Degraves Street, Hobart: in use between 1828 and 1856. Built on the site of an old rum distillery, it was designed by John Lee Archer. During its years of use, 3,705 female convicts spent time within the walls. After 1856 it was transferred to the local authority and ceased to be used as a female factory but continued as a prison. From 1879, it was first used as a Contagious Disease Hospital, then as an Invalid Depot. Later it became a maternity hospital but now is a historic site. The Matron's Cottage survives as the only remaining original building.

The Factory had quite a colourful history and some incidents stand out. In 1830, the Factory was visited by the governor of Van Diemen's Land and his wife. They were entertained on the day by the Reverend William Bedford, a well known hypocrite. When he began to deliver a sermon, three hundred women turned their backs on him, pulled up their clothes and showed their naked bottoms which they also smacked with their hands making a loud and not very musical noise. The governor and other males were not amused but the ladies in the party showed their sympathies with the convict women and laughed out loud. On another occasion, Bedford was grabbed by about 15–20 women and stripped of his clothes.

George Town Female Factory: opened in 1829 but was used only for a short period as another factory was opened in Launceston in 1832. The George Town Factory was situated in a cleric's house.

1829 – George Town Female Factory – Rules and Regulations

The dress of the females shall be made of cheap and coarse materials, and shall consist of a cotton or stuff gown, or petticoat, a jacket and apron with a common straw bonnet of strong texture; and the classes shall be distinguished as follows:

The First Class shall wear the dress without any distinguishing mark.

The 2nd class by a large yellow C on the left sleeve of the jacket.

The Third Class by a large yellow C in the centre of the back of the jacket, one on the right sleeve and another on the back part of the petticoat.

Each female is to be furnished with clean linen every week:

2 aprons
2 shifts
2 caps
2 handkerchiefs
2 pairs of stockings

The diet of the several Classes shall be as follows:

Breakfast – ¼ lb of bread and a pint of Gruel
Dinner – ¼ lb of bread and a pint of Soup
Supper – ¼ lb of bread and a pint of Soup

(The soup to be made in the proportion of 25 lbs. of meat to every 100 quarts of Soup, and to be thickened with vegetables and peas, or barley as maybe most convenient.)

Launceston Female Factory: opened in 1832. It was reported in the local press in 1833 that the building work was in a very advanced state. Much credit was given to the builder. By 1837, things had changed and the establishment was considered wholly useless and the females held it in the utmost contempt. Something had to be done to check the growing disgust with which convict labour was regarded – especially so as the Colonists had to bear the whole of the police expenditure.

From reports in the Launceston *Advertiser*, September 1842:

Superintendent: Robert Pearson	
Under Colonial sentence	6
Solitary confinement	10
Confined by order of the magistrates	97
Nursing children	10
Sentenced to the washtub	9
Servants, cooks etc	4
In the hospital	13
Women assignable in Launceston	63
Total number of women	212
Children under 1 year of age	36
Children under 2 year of age	4
Children under 3 year of age	1
Children under 2 year of age	1
Total number of children	42

1842 – September Inquest

Another inquest was held on Tuesday, at the Court House, on the body of a child which died at the factory on that morning.

The nurse who attended the deceased stated that the child was apparently in a good state of health until Sunday, when she was taken with a cough, several children in the factory were affected in a similar manner.

Dr Maddox proved that death was occasioned by inflammation of the lungs, which he attributed to the prevalence of the southerly winds for the last few days.

There were upwards of thirty children taken with catarrh in the factory on Saturday night. Other witnesses were called who proved that the deceased had regular attendance, and the usual remedies were had resource to.

Verdict: died by the Visitation of God.

During the following month riots broke out in the Factory. On one occasion the women revolted and took over the establishment. They made an unbearable noise. The place was put under siege and food withdrawn but it had no effect. Thirty men and constables had to fight and overcome them. The leaders were taken to Hobart Town. During another riot, Dr Maddox was wounded.

February 1843 — Fire!

The inmates of the Female Factory were greatly alarmed on Saturday by cries of fire. It appears that some young ladies had been occupying their leisure hours, in endeavouring to smoke out the bugs when some of the bedding accidentally caught fire. Fortunately the damage was sustained.'

'The matter was fully investigated by Captain Gardener on Monday and Tuesday and some who had been culpable were sentenced to fourteen days in confinement.

Yet again in May 1844, further riots broke out on three different occasions when many women barricaded themselves in one of

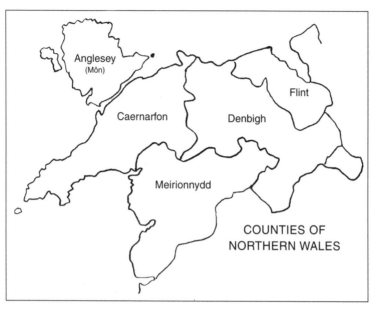

Counties of northern Wales

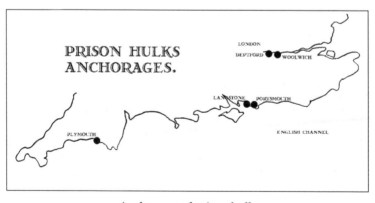

Anchorages of prison hulks

Beaumaris Court House

The dock, Beaumaris Court House

Iron bars to keep out the public: Beaumaris Court House

Legal arguments

Bound for Botany Bay

Restraining iron fetters

Keep shut – always!

*Demoralised, dejected
and downhearted*

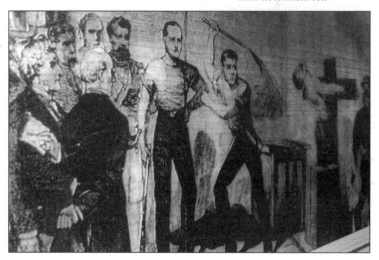

Corporal punishment

Beaumaris gaol

Prison Walls, Beaumaris

Not the most welcoming of places: Beaumaris gaol

To the exercise yard, Beaumaris gaol

Entrance to Beaumaris gaol

'Iron bars do not a prison make ...'

Ruthin gaol

Thirty-eight windows – but no view. Ruthin gaol

Ball and chain used in Ruthin gaol

The bare necessities of cell life: toilet and reading material, Ruthin gaol

Bath and equipment at Ruthin gaol

Prison laundry, Ruthin

Washing facilities at Ruthin gaol

Prison workroom

Typical cell

To move for payment to the Undersheriff of the Sum of £14..2..0 for expenses incurred in conveying Ann Williams from the County Gaol on board the Garland Grove Convict Ship at Woolwich And for preparing Bond for her safe delivery.

Document referring to Ann Williams, who was transported from Beaumaris to London and thence to Van Diemen's Land

Bollard by the Thames in London – the starting point of transportations to Australia

Living quarters on board a convict ship

Sleeping arrangements on board ship

NAME. *Ann Williams* **No.**

alias Ann Edwards

Trade.........................*Farm Servant, Milk & Wash*

Height(without shoes)....*5/1/2*

Age...........................*19 years*

Complexion................*Fair*

Head.........................*Round*

Hair..........................*Lt Brown*

Whiskers..................

Visage.......................*Round*

Forehead...................*Low*

Eyebrows...................*Lt Brown*

Eyes.........................*Hazel*

Nose.........................*Long*

Mouth.......................*Medium width*

Chin..........................*Round*

Native Place..............*North Wales*

Remarks...................*Face pockpitted (slightly)*
Small cut on right thumb.
Two moles on wrist (left)

*Description of
Ann Williams,
from Tasmanian
'Black Books'*

Gegin Filwr, Llanfechell, Anglesey

Cae'r Mynydd, Llithfaen, Gwynedd

In Memoriam – Robert William Hughes, transported 1813

The old Caernarfon Gaol now houses county offices

The harbour, Trefor, with a steamer being loaded with sets and the sailing ship Jane and Ann *waiting to load. In 'Doc Bach' can be seen one of the sailing ships which used to carry stones to the goal at Caernarfon for the prisoners to grind.*

the rooms. All were punished by hard labour.

From the July 1844 papers comes a description of a factory marriage. When a marriage had been approved by the Governor, the woman in question was allowed to walk around the town with her friends. Many marriages were suspicious and it was noted that the system was in need of alteration and improvement. Many got married as soon as possible after arrival, but in reality they waited only to be chosen by a male convict. They would stand in a row outside the factory, as in a hiring fair, and wait to be noticed and chosen. When chosen, the man would drop a handkerchief on the ground in front of his intended. If it was picked up, it was a sign to arrange a marriage as soon as possible. Had she left a husband behind in Britain, she was meant to wait for seven years before re-marrying but one method of overcoming such a rule was to live together outside wedlock or 'over the brush'. Though this kind of arrangement was frowned upon by the authorities they encouraged marriage to populate the new country, so they usually turned a blind eye to any unofficial ceremonies.

The factory buildings were demolished in the 1930s and a college built on the site. Only the well and perimeter wall remain.

Ross Female Factory: opened in 1847, adapted from an 1842 Road Gang Station, which was used by male convicts. It was also used as a nursery but due to poor diets and unhygienic conditions, it had a very high infant death rate.

All the factories and penal settlements had differing reputations, but the one thing they all had in common was that they were considered places 'where evil is constantly perpetuating and increasing itself' where nothing better than'… vegetative misery for all …' was offered. In fact, no-one grieved their passing.

Chapter 6

Convicts sent to hell

I was the conscript
Sent to hell
To make in the desert
The living well.
      (*Old Botany Bay*, Mary Gilmore 1918)

At the beginning of the nineteenth century there were roughly two hundred offences carrying the death sentence. Amongst them was Grand Larceny, or stealing goods above the value of 1/-. Often, juries declared the value of any stolen items to be less than 1/- so as to reduce the charge to one of Petty Larceny, which did not carry the death penalty but could, and often was, punished by a sentence of transportation.

'. . . to Hell' from Anglesey
Hugh Morris alias Jones was a labourer from Ceirchiog, Anglesey who was caught stealing clothes and property belonging to Richard Roberts of Llangristiolus. Hugh was sentenced to be transported for seven years on 6 August 1801.

Twenty years later, in 1820, John Hughes was found guilty of stealing a heifer worth £5 belonging to William Thomas. He was originally sentenced to be 'launched into Eternity'(sentence of death), but after much consideration the verdict was changed to one of transportation for fourteen years.

John Nicholas alias Nicholls, a butcher from Llanffinan, near Llangefni, Anglesey knew of the penal system and had first-hand experience of the risks he took when breaking the law. He

82

had been in prison once already. Even so, he appeared in court on 5 May 1821 and confessed that one of Moses Williams of Llansadwrn's sheep was the first thing that he had stolen – since his release from prison! The original sentence of death was transformed to one of transportation for life.

Norris Matthew Goddard had eleven silver spoons in his possessions until they were stolen by John Jones, a labourer from Holyhead, who pleaded guilty to stealing the items of the value of £2 and was transported for seven years.

On 20 February 1829 William Jones, a labourer of Llanfair yn Neubwll was found guilty of stealing five ewes and five wethers (castrated rams) from the flock of Richard Jones of Llanfaelog. He was sentenced to be hung, but was pardoned and transported for life. Whilst waiting for a ship to Australia, William was held on board the hulk *Justitia* at Woolwich on the river Thames in London.

A report in the *Caernarvon and Denbigh Herald*, dated 23 March 1833, states that:

Owen Jones was indicted for stealing money and other articles from the dwelling house of Hugh Lewis. The prisoner was living as farm servant with the prosecutor Hugh Lewis at Ty'n y Bwlch in the pa. of Llanddyfnan. His master at 4 a.m. on the 3rd Sept. directed him to go and fetch the cart for the purpose of carrying in the corn. He himself got up at 5 and upon getting up he missed his shoes, and found on examining his box that four sovereigns and 24 shillings and 6d. had been abstracted from it. The prisoner was pursued and apprehended between Barmouth and Dolgelley. He had on then a coat and waistcoat, trousers and hat belonging to the prosecutor and delivered up part of the money to the constable. The prisoner had been nearly a year in his master's employ and according to his testimony had behaved himself very well during that time.

Members of the Anglesey gentry who made up the jury found him guilty and sentenced him to be transported for life.

In 1835, Richard Edwards, a labourer who used to live in the parish of Trefdraeth, was transported for life after being found guilty of stealing a purse of gold coins belonging to John Williams, Tyddyn Oliver, Trefdraeth. A bag or purse of gold coins seems to imply a considerable sum of money, and what Richard stole was certainly that. His haul was one of 34 pieces of gold coin of the realm called Sovereigns and a further six gold coins of the realm called Half sovereigns and a leather bag. Converted to today's values this would be worth between £1631.70. On being apprehended at the Penmaenmawr Turnpike by Richard Jones of Bangor, He was asked:

'Are you not a sad fellow to steal the man's money?'
Edwards answered, 'I cannot help it now.'
'How did this happen, my lad?'
'Indeed, I do not know.'
'When did it happen?'
'The night before.'
'How did you open the chest?'
'With a 'carthpren'.' (a small paddle or plough cleaner.)

In August 1836, £13 was granted by the authorities to clear the cost of taking Samuel Hughes from Anglesey to the hulks in London to await transportation after being found guilty of stealing. In that same year, William Donnelly and William Davies pleaded guilty to three indictments charging them with obtaining money under false pretences by means of forged passes from overseers of the poor. They were sentenced to be transported for seven years each. Although an account of the trial appeared in the *Caernarvon and Denbigh Herald* at the time, it was only a very short paragraph. Could it be that a sense of shame was felt as the 'poor' had been taken advantage of for 'ill-gotten gains'? Or was it that Donnelly, as his name suggests, was not a local man and that his story would be of little interest to the paper's readers? It cost £24 to take them from Beaumaris to the hulks.

Many, if not most, of the Anglesey criminals have been described as labourers, and though William Williams of Llangadwladr has been described as such, there is a widely held belief that he was also a schoolmaster in a National School on the island. Whatever his circumstances and qualifications, he also had 'slippery fingers' (or 'hairy hands' (*llaw flewog*), as thieves from Anglesey are said to have). He was found guilty of stealing and slaughtering a ram worth 35/-, belonging to Owen Roberts. He was sentenced to be transported for life, later reduced to a term of ten years. William was aided and abetted by Griffith Jones, another labourer of Trefdraeth. Both appeared in court on 5 May 1840.

In the case of John Parry, a labourer from Llanddaniel Fab, the judge was most undecided as to who was guilty as there was 'gross and wilfull perjury on one side or the other'. The case centred on the fact that one promisory note for £17 and one note for the payment of £17, property of John Williams had been stolen. Who else was involved and what exactly had happened, we shall never know, but John was adamant in his own defence before the Court: 'I have nothing to say but this, I paid the money honestly to John Williams and he gave the receipt to me. I have nothing to say other than the truth.' However, he was sentenced to be transported for seven years in 1840.

Both Acts of Parliament – 39 and 40 Geo. II – made it an offence to have on one's person any item marked with an Arrow', i.e. property of the Armed Forces. John Owen's mistake was to be caught, tried and found guilty of stealing a sheet of copper, a copper bolt, hammer and dowelling machine from Her Majesty's Stores in Holyhead. He probably thought that the items would not be missed as such a store was a busy place, with ships in need of repair and renovation etc. sailing in and out of the harbour daily. However, he was punished with transportation for between seven and fourteen years in 1844.

Owen Jones, a butcher from Llansadwrn had a string of offences to his name. He was first convicted of a felony on 5 April 1842. Details of a second document (20 June 1845) note that Owen stole three sheep worth 30/- belonging to J. and H. Williams, and that he was transported for ten years. According to a third document (5 July 1845), he was a resident of Menai Bridge and was found guilty of stealing a wether belonging to H. Williams, Bryn Eryr, Llansadwrn – a tenant farmer. It is also stated that he was guilty of the previous theft. The jury took their time in reaching a verdict as they deliberated from half past eight till half past midnight and it was only then that the judge passed sentence – transportation for ten years.

An Amlwch resident, Ellis Roberts, became an Australian convict for seven years after being found guilty and transported, in 1848, for stealing two sheep belonging to Hugh Roberts. He was also guilty of stealing a sheep from Rowland Roberts for which he was sentenced to one week's further imprisonment.

On 23 March 1850 Thomas Smith of Aberffraw and John Evans were found guilty of stealing a watch and a pair of shoes from Owen Lazarus of Llanfihangel Tre'r Beirdd. Both were transported for seven years. Smith was a married man with one child but was sent out regardless on the *Pyrenees*. In Western Australia he had little time to earn a living as a butcher. Sadly, he did not live long in exile and two months after arriving there he died on 5 July 1853.

In 1850, John Thomas/Roberts became another transportee from Anglesey to Australia. He was a sheep rustler who was transported for seven years.

According to the 1851 Census, Alexander Gough was in Beaumaris Gaol. His details include the facts that he was born in 1817 in the Shields district of Northumberland and that he was unmarried. His occupation was noted as that of a 'coal miner'. On 19 March 1856 he was charged with breaking and entering and stealing a shirt – the property of John Lewis of Llanddyfnan

– but was found not guilty. Described as a determined criminal – he was once more in court on 27 July of the same year, on a similar charge of breaking and entering and stealing a shirt, the property of John Thomas of Erw Bont, Llanbedrgoch – Gough had been stopped on the Bangor side of the Menai Bridge with the shirt stuffed in his bag. In his statement to the court, he said:

> All I have got to say is that, I was walking along the road on Monday morning with a young man, and we met with a man on the road and he forced us to go into a Public House to get beer, and then forced us until we got intoxicated in liquor and when we came back he forced (me) to go to this place and it was against my heart to do it ... I have nothing to say.

His sentence was one of fifteen years' transportation. On arrival at the Swan River Colony, Western Australia, on 1 June 1858 his occupation had changed to one of an engine driver. He earned his Ticket of Leave by 17 December 1860, but had to wait until 15 February 1872 to be granted his Certificate of Freedom in Champion Bay. In later years, he earned his keep as a labourer and hut keeper.

On 11 September 1856, George Williams pleaded not guilty whilst his partner James Healy pleaded guilty to the crime of stealing a green cloth cape, the property of Hugh Williams, Menai Bridge. Hugh's wife, Jane, had left the cape on a bush to air, though why it was stolen is anybody's guess, as Jane herself said in court that she had left it on an elder bush owing to the moths having got at it. Healy, as he stated in court, was under the influence of alcohol but the cape was later found in a bundle in his possession at Bangor. Healy, to his credit, said, 'I know that Williams knows nothing about the cape, for he had gone up the hill before me and I followed shortly after with a female'. Williams said, 'On Wednesday evening, my wife went away and I went to seek her to Menai Bridge and met Healy the other side of the bridge'. Both men severally offered up pleas for mercy on the grounds of a full determination to avoid crime for the future. Healy stated his readiness and capability to serve as a sailor and attributed his crime to the sheer want of dress. He was, however, well-clad. Both were found guilty of the crime despite their protestations, and were sentenced to be transported for fifteen years. On hearing his sentence, Healy threw something at one of the witnesses, and there being symptoms of insubordination in Williams and Healy, they were ordered to be removed in irons. Order was not maintained without much aid from the police. The commotion that they caused only served as an opportunity for the officials to remind the court that they had a previous conviction for Highway Robbery. Australian records show that Williams was sent out on the ship *Edwin Fox*. The ship arrived on 21 November 1858 with Williams, a Protestant, semiliterate, married carpenter on board. He was granted a Ticket of Leave on 9 April 1860, and apart from the fact that he lived in the Perth area, nothing else is known of him or what became of him. His partner in crime is also listed among the Swan River Colony prisoners and the details found match what was reported in the north Wales newspapers. Healy is described as an unmarried Roman Catholic. His occupation is listed as a butcher and he is credited with being literate. A Ticket of Leave was granted him on 25 April 1860.

'. . . to Hell' from Caernarvonshire

Henry Bicknell of the Penrhyn Arms, Bangor dealt only with South Down and Leicester sheep, which are quite different from the ones that wandered the slopes of Eryri and around Llanddeiniolen in 1836. Evan Owen was no expert, and the two lambs he stole from the Penrhyn Arms flock stood out as being obvious misfits amongst the sheep of Evan Roberts. Roberts said that he had been given the lambs in lieu of money owed him by Owen. Owen said he had bought the lambs from a man in a public house, but he could not recall who or where! If he had been able to remember, the man in question might have been able to save him from a sentence of transportation for life.

'You are to be transported for seven years to such parts of her Majesty's penal settlements as the privy Council would deem fit' were the words heard by Cornelius Orme/Owen on 6 January 1838 as he was sent down for his part in stealing seven sovereigns, seven handkerchiefs, a waistcoat and other articles the property of William Hoys or Evan Williams. Williams was master of a vessel that arrived at Beaumaris, Anglesey on 9 December 1836. When the prisoner was found at Pwllheli, he said to John Dodd, the arresting police officer, 'Well, the job's done. I can say nothing to it.' The judge further commented, 'You have been guilty of a gross breach of trust.'

John Dodd was again the arresting officer in the case of John Edwards, who broke into and entered the house of David Thomas, Waunfawr. He stole 20 sovereigns and when arrested was found to have on him a pair of scissors with identical marks to those left on the window frame of the house he had broken into. Despite pleading to the court that he and his wife had only 1/2d. in the whole world, he was, in turn, described as an itinerant tinker and an umbrella maker, who had a career of fraud, theft and vagabondism, and transported for fifteen years.

For stealing clothes from Robert Roberts and a timepiece belonging to Richard Parry, Henry Hughes was sentenced in 1838 to a month's hard labour. When that sentence had been served, he was further punished by the Assize Court by being transported for seven years. It cost the authorities £12 for him to be taken to the hulk *Justitia* moored at Woolwich.

On 11 December 1855, for falsely pretending to David Jones that he was the servant of Evan Griffith, Chwilog Fawr, Llanystumdwy, and that he had also been the servant of Evan Griffith's brother by whom he was owed money, and for unlawfully obtaining from Jones four yards of cloth to the value of 24/-, twenty-five yards of woollen card to the value of 13/9, one waistcoat piece value of 7/-, one black silk handkerchief value of 6/-, and falsely pretending that Griffith would pay for them,

William Williams was transported for four years. He was a prolific thief as proved by the fifteen other documents to focus on
his life of crime at the Archives.

'. . . to Hell' from Meirionethshire

If intent on stealing anything, it should be of the utmost importance that the stolen items cannot be traced back to its original
owners. Alas, William Williams alias William Peacock did not
take such care, and the horse he stole from Rev. Humphrey
Lloyd of Bala in August 1835 was easily traced and tracked back
to his home stable as it had a peculiarity on one foot. His lack of
thoughtfulness cost him his freedom for life.

'. . . to Hell' from Flintshire

The benefits of education were not available to everyone in the
early nineteenth century (1837), but it could well be that William
Davies of Wrexham was able to read as he stole six books from
Mr. Russell's school, as well as a gig harness belonging to Mr.
Taylor of The Pigeon Inn. For the first offence he was sentenced
to six weeks imprisonment and for the second – transportation
for seven years!

Edward Davies (aged twenty-six), of Wrexham, stole £5 from
the person of Daniel Jackson, Llan y pwll, a farmer with ruddy
cheeks. Daniel had been drinking since before breakfast at The
Coach and Horses. He had spotted an identifying mark on his
£5 note but was so drunk he did not notice what was going on
around him. On buying a round of seven gins and water at
around 5 or 6 o'clock, he had waved the note but was so inebri-
ated he did not notice it was missing until the morning after the
night before. All he found in his pocket was a copy of the pop-
ular song 'Jolly Joe'. Though of good character, Davies was
transported for seven years.

James Evans stole a sheep carcass from Thomas Price,
Wheatsheaf, Wrexham on 19 March 1843. It was a marked carcass and was eventually found in the prisoner's dwelling place,

whilst he was arrested 60 miles away in Stoke on Trent. On sentencing him to be transported for twelve years, the judge reminded him that he had been twice convicted of serious offences, been leniently dealt with, and received a mild sentence. Clemency had been abused and he was not allowed to stay in this country to repeat the offences.

On a cold, windy, freezing day Thomas Jones had been seen walking about to keep warm and complaining he had no money. Suddenly, he was seen wearing a shirt but it was recognised by its maker – Elizabeth Jones – because it had a peculiar button on the collar and as being the property of John Ellis, Pontnewydd, Flintshire. Because he had a previous conviction, Thomas was sentenced to be transported for seven years on July 1 1843.

Catherine Evans visited Wrexham in 1847. From Welshpool originally, she had gone to Wrexham to meet her sister. She hoped to return by railway but having lost her way, she was found by John Jones who dragged her up a lane pretending it was a short cut to the station. He stole 7/6 from her and threatened to kill her with the penknife he had also stolen. Catherine Williams, John's sister, gave a rambling statement to the court but was ordered to leave the witness box as what she had to say had no relevance. His father could not account for the movements of his son on the night in question so he (John) was transported for seven years.

'. . . to Hell' from Denbighshire

In 1845, the punishment for stealing one donkey merited 14 days in prison but Ishmael Davies of Llangynhafal stole five donkeys from Richard Parry. One of the donkeys was recognised because of peculiar marks on his coat and had been sold to a Sarah Roberts for 10/-. Poor Ishmael was transported for seven years.

William Barton and Edward Jones had been in Ruthin Gaol for five months before appearing in court on 10 January 1852 on a charge of stealing 50 lbs of lead from George Harries' roof. Both had hidden their loot in a sack in a field but were seen by PC John O'Donnell returning to their lair. He could not apprehend them as he did not have a warrant. The lead was found in a field and was compared to the gap on the roof of the house it had been stolen from. Shape and size matched perfectly. Both prisoners asked why the court should accept the word of a policeman about lead as they thought the best person for that job was a plumber! Ten years transportation was added to their original prison sentence.

One who was sentenced to be transported for six years on 18 October 1856 professed to be pleased that he was going. 'I shall now be transported for life and if I am not now, I shall be, and would rather be in that country than in this.' That was how Thomas James responded to his sentence after being found guilty of stealing 6/6 from William Jones, a sawyer who had fallen asleep in the Cross Keys public house. On awakening from a drunken stupor, he found his money missing and that James had dipped his hand in his pocket.

Chapter 7

Convict maidens

'And wretched is the Convict Maid.'
(The London Convict Maid)

Many of the women who were sentenced to be transported to Australia were labelled as prostitutes and whores. It is difficult to believe that all the young girls and women from north Wales were of that social grouping. They might have been found guilty of theft, but it is doubtful if they were purveyors of 'the oldest trade', as few references to that particular calling can be found in court documents kept at the Archives.

Some girls became prostitutes during the voyage and after arrival. Many prisoners who were mere girls were sent out deliberately, at the behest of the Beauchamp Committee, because of their age. This was a policy strictly adhered to for a number of years according to Deirdre Beddoe, who plainly states that 'There is ample evidence to confirm that the main reason women were transported was for the sexual gratification of both free and convict males.'

Many transported females were considered to be 'low class women, foul mouthed and with loose morals'. If something went missing in an upper-class house, the servant was generally blamed, and often could be convicted, sometimes without evidence.

At a time when transportation was a regular punishment a rhyme of the period said:

The law locks up the man or woman
Who steals the goose from off the common,
But leaves the greater villain loose
Who steals the common off the goose.

It could well be that the sentiments expressed were just as true of north Wales as of any other part of Britain at that time, and the poets of the day were not the only ones to suspect 'that many of those who have been sent out have been driven to commit the offence for which they have been sent out through want' – a view made public by none other than Sir George Arthur, Governor of Van Diemen's Land in 1837. Many of the ones who appeared in court were driven almost insane by hunger and need of the basics of life.

One such prisoner was Sarah Owen, an unmarried woman from Llangefni, Anglesey. She suffered a fate worse than any sentence the courts could impose on her. Being found guilty of stealing four pillow cases worth 1/-, two linen sheets worth 6d, two towels worth 6d, and two caps worth 2d – the property of Owen Thomas of Llanrhwydrus, and of taking belongings of Margaret Owen and Elinor Williams, both of Llanfairynghornwy, on 22 May 1807, and sentenced to be transported for seven years appeared to be the least of her problems. She may have been thought of as a prolific thief who fully deserved her punishment – but Sarah never left Anglesey. In 1809 an application for her to be pardoned was sent to the authorities by Mr. O. Owen, surgeon, as Sarah, by then, was insane. Such was the effect of her sentence.

Anglesey Maidens
Catherine David Ellis, of Beaumaris was well known by more than one name – alias Owens, widow; alias Elin Davies – unmarried. She broke into the house of John Jones, an Aberffraw farmer. Her haul from the house included: six silk handkerchiefs; one cotton handkerchief and a pair of gloves

worth 25/-. The original punishment was the death sentence, but she was pardoned for her crimes and transported for fourteen years. The Court Authorities allowed a sum of £30 to Thomas Jones, captain of the brig *Esther*; to convey Catherine from Beaumaris to Millbank Gaol, London.

In 1827, Catherine Williams stole a purple glass cream jug, worth 1/3d, one chamber pot worth 5d. and a hat worth 3/6d. She stole the said items and was caught. After an appearance in the Quarter Sessions she was sentenced to be transported for seven years. She joined another convict in Beaumaris Gaol who was also awaiting transportation – John Roberts.

Prisoners' Names	When brought Cause or Offence into Custody		How Subsisted
Catherine Williams	15 Nov. 1827	Under sentence of Transportation for Larceny	Spinning
John Roberts	13 Feb. 1830	Under sentence of Transportation Felony	4d pr day County Allowance

A Kalender of prisoners in the Common Gaol of the County of Anglesea this 20th day of April 1830.

It cost £15 9s. (£764.62 in 2010) to convey John to the hulks at Woolwich. (An enquiry from Whitehall to Beaumaris about the costs of transferring prisoners from the county to London showed the total cost for 1828 to be £30 4s. 4d. John left England for New South Wales in 1831 aboard the convict ship *York*. In the Australian records, he is described as an unmarried ploughman/shepherd.)

Though much of what she had stolen had been recovered, it

was of no beneficial consequence to Margaret Williams, a maid/servant, as she was sentenced to be transported for life in 1837. It is doubtful, though, that she saw Australia as the court recommended Mercy as she was 'weak in intellect'. Her employer – William Edwards of Castell, Llanidan – had left her at her workplace but when he and his family returned home, they found that money and property worth £5 was missing from the cupboard where they were usually kept. William knew his servant well and made his way to the ferry at Tal y Foel, on the Menai Strait, as he guessed that she would be making her way home to Caernarfon. She was found with two bundles of clothes and, hidden in her bonnet, 29 gold sovereigns and 30/- in silver.

Anne Williams (alias Edwards), seventeen years old, from Gegin Filwr, Llanfechell, Anglesey was the second of three children of William and Mary Edwards of Y Gegin Filwr, Llanfechell, Anglesey. William was employed as a carrier working from the nearby Mechell Mill. To have his daughter appear in court on a charge of stealing milk from a cow in a field (her first offence) was shameful enough as the family may well have had their own supply of milk, but for Anne to appear in court twice more must have been heartbreaking. By March 1841 she was in Court, again, accused of breaking into the dwelling house of Hugh Hughes of the parish of Llanfechell on 21 February and stealing five knives, value 2s., five forks, value 2s., 1 lb. soap, value 6d, 2 pairs sugar tongs, value 1s, and articles of clothes. She was found guilty and imprisoned for six calendar months with hard labour.

Her third appearance was for stealing 'wearing apparel' from a dwelling house. 'The prisoner pleaded not guilty of the charge of having feloniously broken into the house of Thomas Hughes at Llanfechell on 27 February 1842 and stolen there from two cotton gowns, a pair of stays, a silk handkerchief and several other articles of wearing apparel'. In her defence, the prisoner stated that Thomas Hughes had given her the clothes. She had no witnesses of his giving her the clothes, but plenty could speak to his being in the habit of visiting her. No witnesses, however, responded to her call. She was taken from Beaumaris to London and transferred to Millbank Prison before being moved onto the *Garland Grove*. The ship began her second convict-carrying voyage on 2 October 1842 from Woolwich, and arrived in Van Diemen's Land on 20 January 1843. According to a message sent to Elizabeth Fry, the prison reformer, by Miss Elizabeth Lang Grindod, 'ship arrived safely after an agreeable voyage of 110 days.'

On arrival in Van Diemen's Land, everyone was put to work. Females were usually sent to factories which were part of a workhouse complex. Because of troublesome behaviour Anne had to spend ten years without a Ticket of Leave before being released in 1853. She found it difficult to obey the rules, and documentary evidence from Tasmania states that she was quite a thorn in the authorities' side. More than once, the record states that she was:

absent without leave
disobedient of Orders & Indolence
took Spirits into the House
absent a day & night without leave
puncheous
absconded
had a Man Improperly with her on her Masters Premises
delivered of an Illegitimate
disrespectful
disobedient of Order
long of a neglect of duty

Her punishments included:

10 days Solitary
14 days Solitary Confinement
3 months hard labour added to her sentence

3 months hard labour in the House of Correction
admonished & returned to Governor
6 days Solitary Confinement

What else is known from detailed Tasmanian records is that Anne Williams (*Garland Grove*) and George West (free man), both residing in the Morven area, were married in December 1847. George was from Edinburgh, Scotland. Apprenticed as a carpenter who specialised in cart making, he was caught with his brother John and a group of other boys, stealing from a sweet shop in Aberdeen. He also pinched the Poor Box, and was sentenced to be transported for fourteen years, 'for the further good of a bad character', by the prosecutor Alex Miller. When his term of transportation ended, George changed his name to Couth West. They raised a family and lived their lives quietly. George died in 1872; Anne's death was on 14 January 1890.

Mary Owen, also known as Lewis, of Amlwch, was convicted of stealing various items of material, consisting of a muffler, gown, a piece of ribbon and other articles belonging to John Hughes (shopkeeper) on 7 November 1848 and sentenced to be transported for seven years. Though she pleaded not guilty to the charge, there were witnesses willing to testify against her in court. Ann Hughes, wife of John, said that the prisoner used to come into the middle of the shop without ringing the bell although cautioned not to do so. One witness said that she had bought 'stuff' from the prisoner's mother for 2/-, which the mother had sold as she needed money to buy food for breakfast for herself and Mary. Mary herself:

confessed to being in an unhappy condition which forced her to receive presents from young men and the articles in question were given to her by some young men whom Margaret Hughes (lodging house keeper, in whose house Mary and her mother stayed) permitted to sleep with her in her house.

In the twenty-first century, the judge would have called for reports from health and social workers before sentencing. Mary was sentenced and sent to Australia.

Another Anglesey Maiden of the same name was Mary Owen/Williams, again from Amlwch was sentenced to seven years' transportation to Van Diemen's Land on 2 January 1849 for stealing, with force and arms:

1 muffler worth 2/-
1 woollen muffler worth 2/-
1 other muffler worth 2/-
1 shawl worth 2/-
1 woollen shawl worth 2/-
1 other shawl worth 2/-
1 Delane muslin worth 13/-
12 yards of muslin worth 13/-
1 piece of ribbon worth 10/-
20 yards of ribbon worth 10/-

all being the property of the above John Hughes. In sentencing her, the judge reminded the court that this was her second offence and that the first offence was still 'in full force strength and effect and not in the least reversed annulled or made void', just in case anyone showed any mercy towards her. Mary was assisted by her mother – Catherine Owen otherwise known as Williams – who was also found guilty. Catherine was spared transportation but had to endure a sentence of Imprisonment and Hard Labour for eight months due, probably, to her age and the fact that she was a widow.

Caernarvonshire Maidens
Lowry Griffith was found guilty of housebreaking and was arrested at her grandmother's house at Dolbenmaen. The victim was a gentleman by the name of Hugh Hughes – a portrait painter. Lowry was transported on 19 March 1836 – for life.

One of the most noted characters of Caernarvon was the cook Mrs. Margaret Presdee alias Prestee alias Prestie alias Preslee alias Begw Dau Ŵr (Begw Two Husbands). She was a regular at the Duke of Wellington public house in town, and it was there in April 1840 that she lifted a man's purse with six sovereigns and a quantity of silver in it. In January 1844 she was in trouble once more, being fined 10/- and 10/- costs for assault. Not having the money to pay, she was imprisoned for a month. She was out and back to her old ways by 28 May 1844, though she was acquitted by the court on a charge of stealing. During the hearing she was given the description of 'a well known nymph of the pavement'. By October 1844, she had appeared at the Quarter Sessions charged with receiving stolen property as the result of a robbery from Richard Owen's drapery shop, Bridge Street, Caernarvon. She had with her a young accomplice, Robert Williams and her attempts to lead him astray earned her this rebuke in the *Caernarvon and Denbigh Herald:* 'Amongst the many modes of extravagance, folly and sin that lead to crime, the sacred moralist has assured us that the company of lewd women is the most dangerous and fearful – ruin, death and judgment are the results of her endearments; and her smile is a yawning sepulchre, engulphing every virtue and every hope.' Margaret was only twenty-two years old when she was transported for seven years, and left in the company of another transportee from her home town.– Morgan James.

Merioneth Maidens

In a rural county such as Merionethshire, the attractions of a town such as Dolgellau must have been a magnet to young girls and women from the outlying villages. Ann Lewis went to Dolgellau and returned with three hats worth £5, a silk shawl worth £10, and an umbrella worth 7/-, from the shop of Hugh Price – all unpaid for. There were also two other girls waiting for their share of the haul. On 13 July 1833 Ann was sent to New South Wales for fourteen years, and her 'fences' – Mary Ellis and

Janet Rees – were also sent there for life. According to a newspaper report, 'The severity of the sentences seemed to create a great deal of surprise amongst the auditors and the prisoners cried most bitterly.'

Ruth Roberts of Bala, went into the garden of Dr Owen Richards to steal four cabbages. She was caught by Evan Evans, a servant, in the back yard of The Goat, and although she pleaded with him not to, he called the police, who were able to match the cabbages with the stalks in the garden. Ruth had a previous conviction for stealing a clockmaker's cutting snippers and was transported for seven years. Whilst on the prison hulk *Anson* awaiting transportation, she was found guilty of 'trafficking in dispensing her wedding ring' and punished with an extra month's probation. She was granted a Ticket of Leave in 1851 and a Pardon in 1853.

Elizabeth Davies and her father did their own detective work for a whole weekend trying to solve a crime of the theft of hats, caps, gowns and an apron from the lodging house where they were staying. Elizabeth and her father followed Eleanor Jones of Trawsfynydd and searched Penrhyndeudraeth on Saturday, Llanfrothen on Sunday, and as far as Dolgellau on Monday, where Eleanor was found wearing the stolen outfits. She was chased by the police and caught and appeared in court in May 1850, where she was sentenced to be transported for seven years.

On 7 July 1865, the Dolgellau court sent Alice Morce to Australia for six years. Described as 'a poor creature with white lips; calling herself a domestic servant', she was found guilty of arson and setting fire to a hay stack. She was the fourth person on that particular day to be transported for arson.

Flintshire Maidens

Amongst pilgrims visiting St. Winifred's Well, Holywell on 10 August 1842 was a Miss Bramian, who had come to bathe and take the waters. When bathing in the sacred waters, she took the precaution of hiding her money under the bed of her lodging house and that is from where Catherine McGrath, her maid, helped herself to £125 in Irish notes and an English sovereign. All this happened at 6 a.m. and Catherine had all day to make her way to Liverpool, where she aroused suspicion when she tried to use a £50 note at the shop of Mr. Hussey. She was sentenced by the court to be sent to Australia for ten years.

Charles Gleaver, a cattle dealer from Burton-on-Irwell, Lancashire, visited Wrexham on 15 June 1847 and went into the Red Cow public house and had three glasses of ale. He then moved on to the Seven Sisters to drink some more. Outside, Mary Tracy, late of Wrexham, propositioned him and asked for a 'treat'. Before he had time to respond, he was held down by two men – who had him by the throat. When they ran off, and Charles had recovered, he found 59 sovereigns and other small change missing. Though Mary insisted she was a stranger to the area and far from her home, she was transported for seven years.

Denbighshire Maidens

For someone earning only a few pennies a week, £15 was quite a sum. Bridget Davies relieved John Jones of Rallt, Abergele of one £5 note (the equivalent of £292.65 in 2010). They met on the night of 17 October 1844 at Llanrhaeadr, as John made his way home. She was sent to Australia for seven years.

Elizabeth Jones met Robert Roberts of Ruthin outside the Prince of Wales public house at 9.30 p.m; smiled at him and asked for half a pint of ale – which he refused saying he had no money. Soon after, he realised that he had been relieved of his purse. Somehow, she managed to find a shoe shop open at that time of night and bought herself a pair of boots. When caught and searched by the policeman's wife, the change from the shoe shop was found on her. On 15 January 1859 she was sentenced to be transported for four years.

Chapter 8

Magpies

The *Pocket Oxford Dictionary* describes the magpie as being a black and white chattering bird noted for thieving. Other descriptions note how the bird would fill its nest with shiny objects such as milk bottle tops or items of gold and silver. Rossini wrote a two-act opera called *The Thieving Magpie*. No wonder, then, that the many criminals found guilty of stealing valuable jewellery and watches were awarded the same nickname.

In researching the court and press records for this chapter, it was found that of those classified as 'Magpies', ⅔ stole silver watches! Silver watches were seen as a sign of wealth and thieves from all over north Wales found them almost irresistible.

After stealing two silver watches from the shop of Michael Hyman at Holywell, on 9 March 1822 Richard Darlington made his way to Chester where he tried to sell them. He was arrested and sentenced to be transported for fourteen years.

Richard David of Bangor stole a silver watch and money belonging to David Owen of Llangoed, Anglesey. Though he protested his innocence, on 8 March 1823 he was found guilty and transported for seven years.

William Tomkins, a labourer of Ruthin, was found guilty of receiving a stolen silver watch, worth £1 15s 6d from Ellen Roberts, who had picked the pocket of Joseph Ferady on 11 November 1826. Both were transported for fourteen years.

John Jones of Saint Asaph had worked out that the best time to break into the house of Mary Williams was when she was in chapel. He stole personal goods, money and two watches, for which he received a sentence of transportation for seven years.

Evan Lewis alias John Lewis of Bangor was found guilty of the 'theft of personal goods including a silver watch and wearing apparel.' Evan and John Jones of Ruabon had stayed the night and shared the same room in the lodging house of Roger Stephens at Rhosllannerchrugog on 31 January 1827. The stolen items and the prisoner were found missing the following morning. Posters were put up offering a reward and he was arrested at the Castle Hotel, Bangor. A sentence of transportation for seven years was passed, and he was taken to await his departure to the hulk *Justitia* at Woolwich, London.

Thomas Metcalf of Holywell mixed with the wrong people when he received stolen copper and brass rings from George Conway, aged fourteen years. Rev. Edward Hughes, clergyman; Henry Bayley Paget, Earl of Uxbridge; David Hughes and Pascoe Grenfil, esq. of the Parys Mine Company prosecuted Metcalf on 1 September 1807 and pressed for a sentence of transportation for fourteen years.

Two criminals, in league, stole silver spoons from the silversmith James Brady of Dublin, Ireland in Holywell, Flint on 3 April 1819. Both William Hodgson and Dennis Nowland were given the same punishment of transportation for seven years.

When Jane Jones, innkeeper of Llangedwyn, Denbighshire found a man hiding under her bed on 6 November 1827 she did not recognise Robert Owen as he was not of that parish. She did, however, recognise a silver cream jug and a sum of money as being her property. Owen was transported for seven years for his crime.

On 31 March 1832 Jeremiah Crawley, a Liverpool 'scally', stood in front of the court at the Denbighshire Assizes and was found guilty of stealing a silver inkstand. He was transported for life. Another with Liverpool connections was John Woodhall, who stole a silver watch and five silver spoons – the property of Thomas Newns of Threapwood, on 2 May 1834. He was arrested at a suspicious lodging house in Liverpool and transported for fourteen years.

Most thieves, when the opportunity arose, made do with one, maybe two watches at the most but Jonathan Jones alias Lewis alias Lewis Wood broke open a safe at the shop of Griffith Davies, watchmaker of Eldon Square, Dolgellau. He had also broken a bar, bolt and latch to gain entry to the shop from which he stole 120 watches, forty gold rings and other property! He was seen by David Jones of Rhydybod, Llanuwchllyn about 22 miles from Dolgellau on the Corwen side of Bala. He was apprehended, tried and on 26 July 1845 he was sentenced to be transported for fifteen years.

Another who had quite a haul on him, when arrested was John Roberts, of Bangor, who was guilty of burglary and stealing a writing desk, silver knife, gold ring, half a crown and two sixpences – property belonging to Ursula Anne Jones – on 2 August 1832, from the house of Dorothea Jones of Bangor. He was sentenced to be transported for life.

Elizabeth Rowlands, a shopkeeper, stole a gold ring from Elizabeth Williams on 28 February 1839. The ring was concealed in a drawer in the house but unfortunately the keys were left in the lock. Witnesses said they saw the keys in the lock and that they were shaking. ER said her goodbyes and left the house in a hurry. The next day, the ring was found in the possession of William Tollman, a watchmaker of Caernarvon. He claimed to have bought it from the prisoner for 2/6 in her shop. Mr. Tollman had cleaned it and offered it for sale in his own shop, according to his testimony. According to Elizabeth Williams' testimony however, she had sold the ring to Mary Williams, a friend of hers, but Mary could not be in court as she was too ill to attend. As Elizabeth had a previous offence to her name – the theft of a cloth cloak from Margaret Jones – she was transported for seven years to such a place beyond the seas as her Majesty's council deemed fit.

Thomas Murry, weighed down by 40 lbs of stolen brass got as far as the George Dock, Liverpool, from the premises of Messrs. Newton, Lyon & Co., Greenfield, Flintshire, on 22

March 1841. He was transported for seven years.

Edward Roberts stole only one silver teaspoon, the property of William Story of the Black Lion Inn, Denbigh. On 22 March 1845, he too was transported for seven years. John McNulty, of Wrexham was given a sentence of transportation for six years for stealing 6 sovereigns. He learnt that the keys to Elizabeth Berkeley's lodging house were kept at the King's Mill Inn, next door. He lifted them and broke in, to steal lodger Rice Jones' money.

Chapter 9

Crimes of violence

Thankfully, not many crimes of violence were recorded in north Wales, and relatively few people were transported for committing such an offence. There are exceptions, though, and there have been such crimes committed in the area over the years. During the 1950s and 1960s the area was thought to be relatively trouble-free; serious crimes were only read of in Sunday newspapers and were thought to happen in large English cities. This peaceful impression was shattered in the 1960s when a murder was committed in Menai Bridge. It became the topic of conversation for worshippers on their way home from chapel on Sunday evenings. Following the case, prison and murderers were used by many an exasperated mother as a threat to unruly offspring, whose longing to go out and play were thwarted by worrying parents thinking that there was many a murderer at large!

On looking at the offences committed by all who were transported from north Wales, it can be seen that most crimes were relatively minor ones. These consisted of stealing farm animals, clothing, food, money and valuables and were probably committed because of want or need. But how does one classify a 'crime of violence'? Living in the early twenty-first century, we have become accustomed to – and indeed are almost immune to – reports of violence in the news. Punishment appears light with the perpetrator being set free in a relatively short time whilst victims and their families have to live with the consequences of such a verdict for a lifetime.

An early reference to a crime of violence is the one from 4

November 1743 when Humphrey ap Richard was sentenced to be transported for seven years. The crime may well reflect the social conditions of the time. Many areas of the Welsh coastline suffered shipwrecks and many a local inhabitant thought it their right to indulge in 'wrecking' – stealing from a wrecked ship. Humphrey was from Llanengan, on the southern side of the Lleyn peninsula – facing the prevailing south-westerly winds which drove many a ship onto the rocks. One ship that came to grief there was the *Kielbauck* of Danzig, Poland. Whatever its cargo, a group of Excise men were sent to guard the ship. Humphrey must have taken umbrage to their presence and was charged with throwing stones at and assaulting William Lloyd, customs officer and his co-workers. He was sentenced to be transported for seven years.

Margaret Evans of Conwy's offence was a much more serious one of Infanticide, in which her female, bastard child was thrown into the town ditch. Although she had behaved honestly and well able three years previously, much can happen in three years and she did in fact kill her illegitimate daughter on 19 September 1762. Her plea of not guilty was refused. She was sentenced to death, pardoned and transported for seven years.

In 1822, Henry Jones of Caerhun, Caernarvonshire was found guilty of stealing from a shop in Llanbedrycennin on 19 December. His haul included money and shop goods. At the scene of the crime a woman's body was found behind the counter. The inquest returned a verdict of murder by unknown persons. Henry's name was not mentioned in connection with this particular aspect of the crime. He was sentenced to death but was later pardoned and transported for life – but the question still remains – did he get away with murder?

Samuel Roberts of Wrexham was tried on a Coroner's Report. The offence was the murder of Jane Woolam. Her death was caused by a blow to the head by an iron bar in her home on 16 October 1825. Sam had often been heard quarrelling with the victim and on the date in question was seen with a cut in his head. He claimed to have been attacked but could not remember who the attacker was! He was transported for life.

Owen Owen of Llanrwst appeared in court on 7 October 1827 on a charge of killing an animal – a horse – which he dispatched of by a particularly cruel method of pouring nitrous acid down its ear. He was transported for life.

The *Caernarvon and Denbigh Herald* of 21 March 1835 carried a report about court proceedings where David Williams of Holyhead was accused of attacking and stabbing William Ruby. Both were sailors on board the packet ship *Etna* – one of the 'mail ships' crossing to and fro from Holyhead to Ireland. It was alleged that Williams had attempted to kill, disable and cause grievous bodily harm to Ruby whilst under the influence of alcohol. He was found guilty and condemned to death, but the sentence was commuted to one of transportation for life.

Another incident on board ship was a manslaughter which became a case of renown in 1836. The incident took place on board an American ship – the *Draco* of Boston captained by William Lincoln – a brig, which was moored off Garth Point, Menai Strait. Newspaper reports describe an attack on the Chief Mate, Isaac Pishion, by an apprentice, nineteen year old James McFall. It was alleged that the apprentice had refused to comply with the mate's orders and a scuffle broke out between the two. MacFall stabbed Pishion in the back and the knife then entered his lungs. The victim was taken to the shore where he was attended by John Roberts, Surgeon. The attacker was seen by the magistrates, charged with stabbing and intent to do bodily harm, and taken to Beaumaris Gaol to await an appearance at the Quarter Sessions. Within five days Pishion died, and the charges were upgraded to Manslaughter. The prisoner was bound over to appear at the next Caernarvon Assizes. Even though he was a prisoner on Anglesey, due to the seriousness of the charge against him the trial was held in Caernarfon during August 1836. The ship's second mate, McQueen, and two other sailors, Issachar Hays and William Hamilton, testified to the court about the alleged attack. Afterwards, in his own defence, McFall testified that he had been subject to a great deal of bullying on board ship and that Pishion had attempted to throw him overboard. He (MacFall) believed that his life was in danger and that he acted in self-defence. In summing up, the judge stated that it was a clear case of manslaughter. The jury dutifully returned a verdict of guilty, but recommended the prisoner to the leniency of the court, on the ground that the manslaughter had been committed under circumstances of great provocation. Later, the prisoner was sentenced to fourteen years' transportation.

MacFall was sent to London on the brig *Robert* but he never arrived. As his ship was sailing up the Thames, close to Erith, on her way to Woolwich, MacFall said he was feeling ill and at sunset, whilst most of the crew were sleeping, he left his bunk, got on deck, took a lifejacket and lowered himself overboard into the river. He floated down river for almost a mile till he came to a barge and shouted for help. On being hauled up onto the barge, he explained that he was a Greenwich waterman and that his rowing boat had been sunk by a steamer but that he had managed to save himself and had been in the water for nearly an hour. It seemed a plausible story and the bargeman served him coffee and brandy and allowed him to dry his clothes, before putting him ashore. The crew of the *Robert* had not missed him and when they realised he had gone, it was several hours later and pursuit was useless. A Caernarfon policeman was sent to London in the hope of re-arresting him but failed in his mission. By then, MacFall had four days' start on him and was presumed to be America-bound via Boulogne in France.

On 30 March 1839 it was reported in the press that Peter Warburton, John Owen and William Davies had broken into Hawarden Church and stolen church linen, two Bibles and some bottles of ecclesiastical wine. Warburton had a previous conviction and was transported for life; the others transported for fourteen years. (In 2008, whilst reading of this particular crime, a coincidence occurred in that a chapel in south Wales was ransacked and damaged. Suggestions from members of the public for punishment of the offenders, if caught, included transportation for life!)

As Llanfihangel Dinsylwy, Anglesey was a rural area, it is quite probable that many inhabitants had a shotgun of their own with which they would hunt hares, pheasants and rabbits etc. for their table. Peace in the area was shattered when Hugh Rowlands used his gun for another purpose. A disagreement arose between him and John Hughes, who was only a boy, because John had testified at the Magistrate's Court the previous month against Hugh on a charge of stealing. Hugh pleaded not guilty to a charge of shooting at John and that 'the act was coolly and deliberately perpetrated, the gun having once missed fire, and been again primed with a new detonating cap. The shot with which the gun was loaded being afterwards found.' John stated that the prisoner had levelled the gun at him. Hugh's defence was that he had borrowed the gun from Richard Jones to shoot crows, a legitimate use in a rural area, and that it had gone off at 'half cock'. He had fired to frighten the boy. Evidence given by Evan Owen, police officer, indicated that thirty-two shots had been found in the fence – a mere 21 inches from where the boy stood – and would have passed him at a distance of 4–6 inches. Hugh had also told the officer that had he a 'hint of his coming, he would have been off in the night.'

The hearing was held at the August Assizes 1840 and fully reported in the local press a week later:

His Lordship [Lord Chief Justice – Thomas, Lord Denman] summed up the evidence, with his usual clearness. The jury retired and shortly returned their verdict, Guilty of shooting with intent to inflict some grievous bodily harm. After a suitable admonition, the court awarded ten years transportation for the offence.

It must have been quite a shock for the residents of Llangefni, the central Anglesey town, to learn that a crime of violence had taken place on their doorstep in March 1843. On 25 March 1843, the court building in Beaumaris opened at 9 a.m. and almost immediately was filled with family, supporters and members of the public for the trial of Evan Morgan of Llanddyfnan and Ellis William, who appeared in court and were charged with the manslaughter and murder of William Parry with a sharp instrument or knife on July 14 1842 in the parish of Llangefni. Each was charged with aiding and abetting the other. Both Morgan and Williams, who were said to be of good character and described by witnesses as 'peaceable, quiet, honest, faithful, humane and steady', had been out drinking on the night in question, spending time at, amongst other places, The King William tavern in town. They had stayed there until between 10 and 11 p.m. Morgan had drunk five or six half pints of ale and claimed he was sober. The newspaper said otherwise and claimed he was, like most other men, reluctant to admit that he couldn't hold his drink. On leaving the tavern and being sober, they had walked around the town, and had seen a drunk William Parry walking up the Menai Bridge Road and turning back towards the Castle public house on Church Street. In the presence of others, a scuffle broke out and Parry was found lying in a pool of blood on the pavement. His injuries were, according to John Lloyd, surgeon, a wound three inches deep and three quarters of an inch in length on the back of the neck. The spinal marrow had been penetrated and his death would have been instantaneous. Conflicting evidence was heard in court about the possession of the weapon and also about a blood-soaked handkerchief, together with the fact that the offence had taken place almost twelve months before the matter was brought to court. Messers. Temple and Welsby, on behalf of both defendants, asked for an acquittal due to lack of proof. The judge and jury, however, saw otherwise, and their sentence was one of transportation for life.

Thomas Ellis of Llansilin, Denbighshire, was caught poaching on Sir Watkin Wynne's land was also transported for seven years for assaulting the gamekeeper by striking him on the back of the head, hitting him with a gun muzzle, and kicking him when he was down. The date of Thomas' court appearance was 7 January 1843 and his offences might well have been committed over Christmas. Such matters were not mentioned in the press reports as the evidence was too conclusive against the prisoner.

The case of Mary Jones appears to be a very sad one indeed. She was 'a Baptist dairy maid in her twenties, a fresh-faced girl with a ruddy complexion and freckles', who murdered her illegitimate child – or as the newspaper report bluntly put it on 24 July 1847, 'her bastard child'. Apparently, she had no family to turn to. On sentencing her, the judge said that 'a strongly disapproving community must take its share of the blame.' Mary was transported for life to Van Diemen's Land, where she found work as a dairymaid on a farm.

Michael O'Donnell was of Irish stock, but like many of his countrymen had come over to north Wales to work on the railway. He had a quick temper and was known and seen as a drunk, but not violent. His crime was to stab Henry Jones of Llanbeblig, Caernarvon. Both had quarrelled over a spade and sacked from their post. On crossing the river Ogwen towards Talybont, Henry was stabbed in the back with a cheese knife. Michael accepted his punishment, 'Well, if I have done it, I must suffer for it'. He was transported for ten years.

On 8 September 1848 William Williams of Beaumaris was the victim of a malicious stabbing by Samuel Smith, a thirty-five year old man described in the 1841 Census as a 'mechanic' who lived at the Green, Beaumaris. Smith pleaded not guilty to a charge of 'malicious stabbing with intent to murder, maim and grievously injure'. The altercation took place in Steeple Lane, Beaumaris at half past eight in the evening. According to Elizabeth Hughes, a witness, Smith was 'in drink' and had attacked his victim without provocation. On being sentenced to ten years transportation, the prisoner fell to his knees and begged for mercy. His wife called out, 'Oh, my poor children,' over and over and it was some time before she could be silenced or recovered.

John Lewis killed Thomas Thomas by striking him on the head and beating him with a poker. Both had previously quarrelled at the Red Lion Hotel and had been in a scuffle. Despite his youth and previous good character, Lewis was sentenced to seven years. His shock at such a sentence made him reach for one of his clogs, which he threw at the chairman of the Bench!

From the parish of Llanaelhaearn, on 15 March 1851, Mary Jones was found guilty of the wilful murder of her illegitimate child – Ellen, six weeks old, born in a workhouse. Baby Ellen's body was found in a field on Cae Bach Farm, on the edge of a ditch by Ann Griffith. It was in a slightly advanced state of decomposition and had been there for two or three days, according to the surgeon. Death had probably been from cold and starvation. Mary had been seen walking with Ellen on the way to her mother's house where, she said, the child was to be fostered. Today, Mary would have been seen by psychologists and psychiatrists but in those days no consideration was given to the fact that she might have been suffering from post natal depression. In 1851, Mary of Llanaelhaearn was transported for life.

Today's newspapers seem to glorify in reproducing every gory detail, in colour if possible, but in March 1851 the *Caernarvon and Denbigh Herald* refused to include a report about what happened to Elizabeth Duncan as the editor thought the 'evidence was unfit for publication'. Mrs. Duncan was staying with her husband at the house of Robert Jones in Gyffylliog,

Denbighshire. Another two men shared the loft with them and they were accused of rape. The eldest, William Jones (only nineteen years old) was acquitted, but the youngest – Evan Jones – was later (2 August 1851) found guilty and sentenced to be transported for ten years – despite William giving him a dubious character reference.

Daniel Watkins, a married man with one child, was transported for life for rape and attempted rape. He served ten years of his sentence before being allowed a Ticket of Leave on 8 December 1873. The rest of his life was spent in Toodyay, Champion Bay, Western Australia working as a farm servant. He died on 23 April 1885 at the Freemantle Prison Hospital, due to kidney disease.

James Hawke, a railway worker assaulted and abused Mary Ann Fletcher, a girl under ten years of age in 1852. Hawke slept in the same loft as the girl, her father and others. The offence came to light nine weeks after it had been committed, when the girl complained to her aunt. Hawke laid the blame on the girl and her father for the venereal disease he had caught, but more than one druggist remembered him buying medicine for himself. 'He had a manner unworthy of manhood and endeavoured to taint alike the mind and body of his victim.' His sentence was transportation for ten years.

On 28 July 1860 John Roberts, 'who did not have a strong mind and was of weak intellect and morose disposition' was found guilty of the rape of Elizabeth Wynne, eleven years old, employed as a cattle watcher. His only defence, before he was transported for four years, was that the girl had consented.

David Owen of Llangelynin visited Dolgellau fair in 1862 where he was 'abused and strangled and money taken from his waistcoat.' Thomas Andrews and Mary Ann Caledine ('both hawkers') were arrested for the crime in a lodging house in Rhyl where they became 'violent and abusive and a scuffle ensued.' Andrews escaped and was later recaptured in Prestatyn. The jury at Dolgellau, 'after a few minutes consultation', and on learning that Andrews had previously 'been an associate of thieves in Merthyr Tydfil', sentenced them both to be transported for eight years.

Joseph Hughes, an illiterate, unmarried labourer killed William Kendrick. On his appearance in court in March 1865, he was transported for ten years. He spent the rest of his life in Western Australia, gaining his Ticket of Leave on 2 August 1870 and a Certificate of Freedom on 23 March 1875 at York, WA. His place of residence was Wellington, Perth and he worked as a labourer, general servant, brickmaker, mowing reaper, haymaker and woodcutter. In the same month (March 1865), Thomas Walsh was transported from Anglesey for seven years for murder.

Charles Spencer, aged twenty-seven years, entered a house and used a knife to subdue his prosecutor and for that was transported for life. He travelled on the last prisoner-carrying ship to Western Australia. Less than two years later, on 2 January 1878, he died at Freemantle Hospital of kidney disease.

Chapter 10

Years of hardship, shame and regret

Georgian Britain – from 1714 to 1838 – was a turbulent period when Britain, for most of the time, was at war with France and fought for control of Europe, North America, the West Indies and India. Due to a powerful navy, Britain usually kept the upper hand. It was also a period of change for the working population, when supplies of raw materials were plentiful and new inventions and machinery made Britain an industrialised nation. Many prospered, but for some it was a very difficult time when 'making ends meet' was a priority that many were unable to manage.

A recent study by the historian Derek Wilson states that 1812 can be regarded as 'the WORST year in British History'. Whilst many other years have gone down in history for different reasons, e.g. 1349, the year of the 'Black Death', and 1536, 'a year of tyranny, persecution and revolt', 1812 remains the year of war and revolution. Luddite mobs broke into mills and broke up newly installed machinery. Bad harvests resulted in the highest bread prices ever. George III was in the grip of illness and his son was an unpopular regent. Political unrest ruled to such an extent that the Prime Minister, Spencer Perceval, was murdered in the lobby of the House of Commons. The effects of such events took their time to filter through to the counties of north Wales, but they must surely have contributed to the fact that court appearances and transportation reached alarmingly high numbers and almost erased the memory of the tradition of 'The Land of the White Gloves'.

In every city, town and village, exciting things happened to make the mid nineteenth century one of the most memorable times ever for those who lived in those particular decades. According to E. A. Williams, author of *The Day Before Yesterday*, 'The 19th century [on Anglesey] is characterised by industrial and social changes'. The same could be said for the other northern counties of Wales.

During the early hours of the morning of 20 June 1837, Alexandrina Victoria was told of the death of William IV and she, at eighteen years of age, was queen. Thus began another exciting period (1837–1901) in the history of Great Britain, and a time which influenced most other countries of the world. This was the time when the 'Red' of the British Empire spread almost like wildfire across the Globe.

Some of the main events of Victoria's reign were: at home, the introduction of a postage payment system, Income Tax; a fall in the price of wheat; the Great Exhibition at Crystal Palace; the Irish Problem; and abroad, the Afghan wars; the Indian wars; the opium wars in China, the Crimean campaign, and the Anglo-Boer war.

It can be seen that life was changing at an ever-increasing pace – almost beyond ordinary people's comprehension. In 1851, the population of Wales was 1,163,139. This number had doubled in only two generations. Two out of every three could speak Welsh, but only one out of every five men (and no women) had voting rights. By 1851, only one third of the population were agricultural workers. Agriculture had changed almost completely because of the enclosure of common lands and the use of different breeds of cattle and sheep. Potatoes and grain were the main growing crops; animals were bred for their meat or for dairy products. Eight out of every ten people had turned their backs on the established church and become Nonconformists. This was an exciting time for those whose lives were touched by such developments, but for the poor, 'caught between two stools', as it were, the developments were of little significance. Few could take advantage of a change in circumstances to improve their quality of life and for most there was only work, and a feeling of resentment and hate grew for those who could afford all the latest benefits. Many of the poor working classes looked for an escape through the medium of strong but cheap drink, and alcohol was quoted as being a significant factor in many of the failings of society. Temperance Societies were founded; the first such society in Wales being in Llanfechell, Anglesey in November 1834. A need for more police and prisons was obvious. In 1839 the Rural Constabulary Act was passed as was an amendment in 1840. In 1842, the Parish Constables Act gave each parish council the right to employ parish policemen on condition they were healthy, young, paying local taxes and rates, and had been recommended by the Justice of the Peace. Was it a misfortune to be born at such a time? What did those who governed the land know about having to budget their meagre pennies? They could all easily afford to squander pounds without noticing the loss. 'They are like two nations that have no contact or sympathy. They know little of each other's habits, thoughts and feelings'. That is how Benjamin Disraeli described the two very differing strata of society – the Poor and the Rich. It was, in reality, a simple division. If you were poor, life was always hard, but if you were lucky enough to be one of the rich, life was 'just a bowl of cherries'.

In 1842, an Act of Parliament was passed preventing women, young girls and children under the age of thirteen from working down the coal mines. This was considered to be a very enlightened Act, as it banned the use of children as young as five years of age from working as fan operators in parts of coal mines too narrow for grown men to enter! It also brought to an end the practise of using women and girls to haul full trams of coal to the surface! How very enlightened of Robert Peel's government, but they dared not go any further for fear of upsetting mine owners and losing the support of influential industrialists.

119

Even though, in the twenty-first century, we might look through rose-tinted glasses on the north Wales of two hundred years ago and think of it as a little 'heaven on earth', but was it a place of 'warm coloured stone cottages, with their thatched roofs and climbing roses, with their village green and the inn and the duck pond and the old steepled parish church, with ploughmen in their smocks, a blacksmith in his trusty apron and wives in cheery cotton dresses', as Matthew Kneale said? Or in reality was it a place of 'rows of cottages or hovels of the lowest description ... cottages are very small and crowded together without proper ventilation or drainage. The people are cramped together in the cottages in a manner injurious to health and decency.' (Amlwch as described in the aforementioned *Report on the State of Education in Wales (1847)*. Many of the people living in such poverty fell by the wayside and found themselves on the slippery slope to a court appearance and transportation to Australia.

In terms of simple statistics, it can be seen that four periods appeared to be more difficult than others for some of the inhabitants of north Wales. It was usual for one, maybe two cases per year to have a sentence of transportation passed, but in the four years from 1755 to 1758 a total of twenty-six cases resulted in a verdict of transportation – a rough average of six per year. In another four-year period 1816, 1817, 1818 and 1819 there were thirty-five cases (an average of around nine per year), and in the decade between 1820 and 1830 a total of fifty-seven cases resulted in a sentence of transportation. This begs the question 'Why?' The peace of the usually quiet haven of north Wales was shattered.

Condemnation of any criminal is easy. They have broken the law so they deserve to be punished. But on looking at the offences committed one begins to wonder why these people felt they had no option but to break the law. Some undoubtedly were habitual criminals and it was those that probably picked pockets, and stole money, silver spoons and watches; they were probably the ones who also received stolen property. Stealing cattle hides or a Bible were not the wisest moves to make and committing a highway robbery asked for quite a measure of daring. It may have been foolhardiness that drove one to steal a hogshead of beer or a measure of drink and wine, but most of the offences committed during these very lean years consisted of stealing either clothing or food. Clothing was a necessary item to keep out the cold or just to look respectable in public. Sheep and cattle could be killed and eaten; a horse could be a very valuable mode of transport, but the really desperate stole poultry for their meat and eggs, whilst thefts of bacon, cheese or pork really speak for themselves. Only once was the theft of tobacco recorded, and likewise the theft of coal.

Another offence that shows a need for basic food was the one of poaching. For the landowner, it was probably a pleasure to raise game, but to a needy man it became a free meal – perhaps even more than one – for his starving family – well worth the risk of being caught. Others took part in what the authorities called Food Riots.

Let us look at these periods which had such a high proportion of transportations:

1755-1815

Between 1755 and 1758, the crime committed most often was 'theft' with cloth and wearing apparel the most common items stolen. Also, sums of money up to £2 8s. 6d were taken. One criminal helped herself to a supply of ribbon and lace whilst another stole riding gear. Sheep and horses were also stolen.

Robert Morris of Cwm in Flintshire suffered a break-in in May 1740 when David Evans of Bagillt, William Frumstone and Phillip Anderson of Whitford, and Joseph Gratton and Robert Lucas of Newmarket broke into and entered Morris' house to steal wheat, food and ale to the value of £12 8s 6d. Desperate men, sometimes, have to take desperate measures.

There was one incident of shop lifting, when a hogshead was

stolen from a store house in Eglwys-bach, Denbighshire – the barrel being the work of Elis Roberts, cooper of Llanddoged. (Elis Roberts was a well known figure of the literary world. Under his bardic name of Elis Y Cowper, he was a prolific writer of ballads, religious letters and interludes. As well as carrying out the trade of a cooper he was also a sexton at Llanddoged Church where his duties included bell-ringing and grave-digging. Elis died in 1789.)

What could possibly be called the crime of the year, if not the crime of the decade, occurred on 7 February 1756 at Wrexham. Francis Appleton of Holt Denbighshire, a yeoman, stole cowhides from John Wright, a tanner. The raw, salted, Irish cowhides had been sent over the Dee from Chester to Holt. There, they were to be kept safely until moved to Wrexham on horseback. Appleton moved quickly and took his haul back to Chester, where he tried to sell them, but as his crime had been 'headline news' and that particular item of news travelled quickly from market town to market town, he was caught, found guilty and transported for seven years.

John Evans of Holywell and Richard Griffith of Mold stole animals. One stole a cow; the other stole a horse. John sold the cow at Chester. Richard kept the horse. Both pleaded not guilty. Both were sentenced to fourteen years transportation within six months of each other.

1816-1820

Four years may be a relatively short period but in 1,461 days many things can happen – and much did happen during 1816 and 1819. During the period in question 38 per cent of crimes in north Wales were deemed to be serious enough to warrant a sentence of death – later commuted to transportation for life.

Burglary, breaking and entering enabled the opportunist thief to steal cloth, food, items of silver, money and personal goods. Others stole drink, horses and sheep.

John Roberts, a butcher from Caerhun, Caernarfon knew

only too well how to handle the sheep that he stole from Elis Jones. The meat was probably sold or shared, cooked and eaten. Disposing of the fleece was more difficult and he was caught whilst trying to sell it at the Eagles Inn, Conwy. He escaped from the constables who were taking him to gaol, but was caught a second time at his own house, where he had armed himself with a knife, quite possibly one that he had used on the carcass and one of the tools of his trade. He managed to escape a second time before he was finally caught at Llanbedrycenin.

One has to ask whether Margaret Jones, of Holywell, knew what she was doing on 12 November 1816, when she admitted to being in possession of counterfeit Bank of England notes at Denbigh fair. Had she picked them up or was she holding them for someone else or had she become involved in a scheme that she didn't quite understand? Her servant and husband were implicated during the hearing but it was she, and she alone, that was transported for fourteen years.

Robert Jones of Denbigh was only thirteen years old when he was held in custody for burglary and theft from the house of William Parry, a druggist. Being so young, the accused was sent to a school in London to await his court appearance. Did his time in a London school during 1817 have any effect on him in Australia? After being transported for seven years, it is hoped that he attained maturity at the end of his term and that he was able to make something of his life in a 'new world'.

When reading court papers and documents in the Archives, one often wonders 'What if?' or 'Why?' In the case of Mary Roberts of Llaniestyn, who was charged with killing a sheep with intent, one asks 'intent to what?' Could it be for the wool or the meat or the carcass? We are not told the whole story. Sadly, all we know is that Mary did her deed on 1 July 1817 and was sentenced to death. Her needs must have been great to risk such a sentence on such an apparent small job. But she was pardoned and transported for life.

What command of the English language did Edward

Thomas, of Dolgellau have? Did he know of the expression 'on tenterhooks' and its origin, or were tenter hooks, to him, just something that happened to hold cloth on a frame in the fulling mill? He took cloth from a tenter (frame) belonging to Ellis Roberts of the Llanfachreth Fulling Mill on 11 February 1818. He was duly sentenced to death, pardoned and transported for seven years. What did the chairman of the bench know of life in Australia as to equate it with a capital sentence?

The journey to the July Chester Fair in 1818 was not the most successful one for John Jones, a hosier from Bala. He stayed overnight at Wrexham, but two men took a shine to his wares and lightened his load. Edward Jones and John Morris, both of Wrexham, may have 'found religion' to claim Benefit of Clergy but they were still transported for seven years each.

John Hughes, 'a desperate character' was found guilty of stealing, on 23 April 1819, a heifer worth £5 belonging to William Thomas of Llangristiolus, Anglesey. Because he had gone to England with a drove of cattle, it was six months after the event that the authorities caught up with him, at Pwllheli, where he had, most possibly, gone back to his roots as he was from the nearby parish of Llangian. He was originally sentenced to be 'launched into Eternity' (sentence of death) but after much consideration the verdict was changed in 1820 to one of transportation for fourteen years.

1820-1830

Life has always been hard for ordinary folk and the year 1820 proved no different. At the start of a new decade George IV came to the throne but was forced to take steps to prevent his queen – Caroline of Brunswick – from being present at his coronation. Lord Liverpool's Cabinet was threatened during the Cato Conspiratory – a plan to murder all Cabinet Ministers. The Ministers came to know of the plan and Thistlewood – the leader of the conspirators and four others were captured, arrested and executed.

The decade was also the time when Robert Owen's philosophy became accepted by Parliament and the public at large; Elizabeth Fry's campaign for better conditions in women's prisons gathered pace. Samuel Romilly had striven for changes to the law, but he died before the death sentence had been lifted from 130 offences in 1823. Even so, crime numbers were still high in north Wales. Various offences were repeated, such as theft of money, wearing apparel, cloth, farm animals. Other offences such as stealing coal, food, and meat were committed, which showed just how desperate people were.

Even on a summer's day, Llandudno can be a cold place. What did William Jones think of his home town as he was sentenced to be transported for life on 1 August 1820 for the theft of a sheep from Llandudno mountain. He had obviously planned what to do as the sheep was found with four legs tied together in a cave. A beady eye was kept on the cave and poor old William was caught with the sheep on his shoulders. He managed to escape but was arrested in Conwy in a very unruly state of mind and threatening to kill the constables.

Highway robbery is, these days, associated with dashing, almost romantic figures who stole from the rich and rode away on their fast horses in the night! Was it really so? Jemima Parry of Wrexham was found guilty of highway robbery of a silver watch from John Edwards of Gyffyllie. She was sentenced to death, pardoned and transported for seven years on 31 March 1822.

Others driven by desperation were caught poaching in a plantation in the possession of Sir Edward Pryce Lloyd, Bart, with intent to kill and destroy game illegally at night armed with a gun at Cwm, Flintshire. This desperate man was 26-year-old Herbert Owen. His punishment, like so many others during the decade, was that he should be transported for seven years.

Food and warmth are amongst life's basic needs. Catherine Jones of Abererch, Caernarfonshire, went into the house of Ellinor and John Samuel and stole a newly slaughtered calf.

Both Catherine and her sister, being very hungry, had gone to the prosecutor's house, with the intention of stealing potatoes. They bit off more than they could chew and were sentenced to death, pardoned and transported for life.

Hugh, Richard and John Rowlands of Llanfairfechan broke into a shop in Bangor and stole cloth, tobacco and food. How did their poor parents deal with the loss of three sons when they were transported for life in December 1827?

A cat and a commoner may look at a king but are not allowed to steal his clothes. A labourer – John Jones of Whitford, Flint – looked at the house of Sir Thomas Mostyn on 16 May 1822, liked what he saw and helped himself to some of the wearing apparel belonging to the baronet and his groom. A king sets the law; commoners have to accept that they can be transported for seven years for such a crime.

Sovereigns. Dollars. Tokens. Irish Coins. Promissory note. All these were taken from the house of Edward Morgan, Esq. of Llanasa, Flint on 1 September 1822. The thief was Robert Price of no fixed abode. His punishment was to be transported for seven years.

In April 1824, Jane Griffiths of Pwllheli was charged with having broken into a bedroom of Bryn Adda, Bangor, and stealing items of clothing. According to the details read out in court, she had tried to sell the stolen property but failed only to give it away in return for food. She gave a linseed apron away for food; a shawl in return for bread, and she tried to exchange a finial shawl because she was in want of meat. That should have been enough evidence to show how desperate her situation was but unfortunately, no-one took any notice of the real reason for her behaviour and she was sent, callously, on her way to Australia for seven long years.

Another who was very much down on her luck in 1824 was Charlotte Davies, but who went to her task with gusto as stole thirty-five items of food, money and clothes from Elizabeth Davies of Llangystennin, Caernarvonshire. She shared some of the clothes with her family and friends and used the money to make her way to Liverpool, but was apprehended there and transported for seven years. She was described by Elizabeth Davies as 'a woman of ill-fame who used to wander about sleeping nights in hovels.' Was she really a woman of ill-repute, or just someone down on her luck? She was reported to have told the court, 'I am just famished with hunger.'

Life is a constant battle; good versus evil; young versus old. Let the good and old be represented by Robert Griffith, a farmer of Llanllechid, Caernarvonshire, who was 'about 80 years of age and very helpless'. Let the evil and young be represented by Ellinor Williams of Llanllechid, who stole money from her employer on 13 January 1825. Good can be further represented by the fact that the prosecutor had his guilty verdict but wasn't it evil that she was transported for seven years?

Robert Ruttlegede of Bloomfield, County Mayo, Ireland did not have happy memories of his visit to Anglesey or his overnight stay at Holyhead. During the night of 13 July 1827 wearing apparel was stolen from his carriage kept in the coach house of Thomas Spencer's inn. Their value was only £1 5s. 7d. but enough to send the thief, Richard Jones to Australia for seven years.

On 20 February 1829, William Jones, a labourer of Llanfair yn Neubwll, Anglesey was found guilty of stealing five ewes and five wethers (castrated rams) from the flock of Richard Jones of Llanfaelog. He was sentenced to be hung but pardoned and transported for life. Whilst waiting for a ship to Australia, William was held on board the hulk *Justitia* at Woolwich on the Thames in London.

Chapter 11

In league

Is there honour amongst thieves? Is there safety in numbers? Two of the groups or gangs of thieves who were caught on Anglesey during the nineteenth century would certainly argue against such statements.

Following their appearance at the Beaumaris Assizes in July 1850 on a charge of burglary in Aberffraw, a group of criminals were sentenced to be transported for seven years to Van Diemen's Land: Thomas Davies, aged twenty-nine, Richard Collis, aged twenty-three, John Roberts, aged twenty-six, Thomas Morris, aged thirty-one, and Ellen Davies – aged nineteen – 'a freckled 'nurse girl'.

The Honourable Sir Thomas Noon Talfourd, judge, was satisfied that they were part of a much larger gang of thieving wanderers travelling the country intent on stealing. Their paths had crossed firstly in Newtown, Montgomeryshire. In Beaumaris they were accused of stealing a cheese, ham, sides of bacon, two writing desks, a chest, a Wesleyan charity missionary box, three pairs of shoes and a shawl from the house of William Williams, Selar, in the parish of Aberffraw. According to the judge they were part of a gang of persons travelling the country without any other object than plunder, and though they had not yet arrived at that pitch of depravity as to use deadly weapons on their nightly depredations, it would be his duty to place it out of their power, at least for some time, to continue in their wicked career.

Ellen – who later sailed to Australia on the *Aurora* – had another charge of larceny to answer, but as she was safely on her way to Australia, the judge, in his wisdom, decided not to proceed with the case.

John Owen alias John Jeremiah alias John Hughes, a room-painter of Caernarvon, and his partner in crime, John Thomas alias John Williams, a labourer of Aber in the same county, had a total of five names with which to baffle the authorities. Nevertheless, they were still caught and found guilty of breaking and entering their prosecutor's dwelling house and stealing cloth and money at Llanrhychwyn, Caernarvonshire.

What led to them being caught was that both men were found lying on the ground under a rock in an old quarry at Llansannan, near Denbigh. John Thomas was also in court for another crime committed on the same day – 20 May 1755 – at the house of Anne Thomas, Maenan, Llanrwst. He stole personal goods including a Welsh Bible, whilst Anne went about her business in Llanrwst market. For the three offences, they were sentenced to death but pardoned and transported for fourteen years.

Not many yeomen feature in the list of those transported from north Wales, but one case in Flint on 25 August 1756 saw two such members of the farming fraternity stand before a court on a charge of burglary at the house of William Jones, a butter man of Hope. Thomas and Robert Jones of Dyserth had stolen £2 8s. 6d. Robert fled the scene and made his way to Bala where he kept his reaping hooks or to Dolgellau to work in the mines. Both were sent to north America for fourteen years.

William Foulkes, yeoman, and Samuel Kenison, maltster, may well have known exactly what they were doing when they stole malt from a malt kiln, belonging to Jonathan Moore, brewer, of Wrexham on 28 November 1811. The fact that one was a yeoman and that the other was well versed in the art of brewing strongly suggests that this is so; both were transported for seven years.

The name of Wil Bryan has strong literary connections with Flintshire and has a conspicuous place in the list of characters from the novels of Daniel Owen. A criminal of the same name was found guilty of the the theft of lead in Halkyn in the county of Flint on 5 June 1817. William Bryan and his partner Thomas Williams were both transported for seven years for the offence.

John Jones and Griffith Roberts, both of Penmorfa, Caernarvonshire, were caught stealing oatmeal from the mill at Llecheiddior on 19 February 1818. They were sentenced to be transported for seven years each.

William Evans and Thomas Jones of Hope, on 20 August 1827, stole some cheese. Again, seven years was deemed long enough for them to atone for their crime.

John Watterson, aged thirty-five; Robert Humphreys, aged forty-seven, and Robert Roberts, all of Mold and employees of the Mold Mine Company, were probably family men with families to support and were prosecuted by John Taylor for the theft of coal in November 1829. They were transported: the first for seven and the second two for fourteen years.

The effect that a sentence of transportation had on the ones left back home can only be guessed at, but it surely must have been a heavy cross to bear for the family when a husband or son was sent to Botany Bay, and it must have been almost unbearable for a mother and father to lose three sons at the same court hearing. This is what happened to the Roberts family of Llanfwrog, Denbighshire when their three sons – John, Richard and Robert were each transported for seven years. At around Christmas time 1819, all three were caught entering a close at night, armed, with intent to kill game. Even though the local newspaper was quite ready to publish details of the court cases, no one seems to have asked why the three brothers had been driven to commit the offence.

In 1833, a gang of five poachers, William Williams, John Edwards, William Pierce, John Wynne and Edward Jones were all found guilty of the same offence and sentenced to be transported for fourteen years.

At the same court hearing, David Roberts, Edward Williams

and Thomas Hughes were found guilty of stealing sheep belonging to H. Maxwell, Esq. of Gresford. The one who received the stolen property, David Challoner lost his liberty on being sent to Australia for fourteen years; the others were to lose theirs for life.

One of the few people allowed into a scene of crime these days is an officer or scientist who checks for minute blood samples to test and group. No such sophistication existed in 1836, and even though blood was found at the house of John Pughe Jones, Llanenddwyn, Merionethshire, it could not be proven to be from a hand and head wound of Owen Jones. Jones, Alexander James and a female accomplice named Elizabeth Roberts were known to have stayed together at a lodging house at Dyffryn. They had left early on the evening of 23 February 1836 and returned at 2 a.m. It was noticed that Jones' hand was bleeding profusely but he said that he had been hit over the head with an iron bar by James. Both men were transported for life.

On 26 October 1837 Elizabeth Roberts was indicted for stealing a quilt and blankets from the neighbourhood of Bala. She was transported for seven years. Was she the same Elizabeth Roberts?

An old Welsh proverb states that where the hen scratches, the chick will peck. Robin Jones of Caernarfon – otherwise known as Robin Shôn Gobbler (shoemaker) and William his son were thieves, but not the brightest of thieves. William stole a pair of trousers, the property of William Jones, schoolmaster of Llandwrog. He was wearing the trousers over another pair when caught! His father was found guilty of stealing pieces of leather from a cellar in the house of William Swan, shoemaker of Caernarvon. He confessed his guilt, whilst John Davies alias John Conway, their accomplice, complained that 'All I got from it was a pair of soles for my shoes!' He didn't have much wear out of them as all three were transported for seven years in July 1840.

Inspector Nicholls and a constable in the North Wales Police Force were only doing their job and had no thoughts of monetary gain when they arrested William Jones (aged nineteen years), and James Williams (aged eighteen years). Both had stolen 4 sovereigns, the property of David Owen of Llansanffraid, Glan Conwy, and in doing so, putting him in 'bodily fear'. The outlaws were transported for fifteen years; the lawmen were rewarded with 40/- for the Inspector and a further (but smaller) reward for the constable.

John Fagan and James Dutton (two Irishmen, probably) were in November 1847 in the parish of Trefriw where they broke into and entered a building belonging to Hugh Hughes and stole various items of clothing and accessories belonging to John Edwards of Pant y garw, Trefriw. Alan Edwards, Edward Lamb and Joseph Howell of Tŷ Hwnt i'r Bont, Gwydir, all appeared in court to testify against them. Fagan was found not guilty, but Dutton was sent to Australia for ten years.

On 28 October 1848 Richard Roberts, Job & Samuel Rowland (brothers) and David Jones, all of Wrexham and described by the press as four desperate looking fellows, attacked Thomas Meredith and stole his money. For their crime, they were transported for seven years.

Two years later, another gang of three were in court for assault, robbery, aiding and abetting each other. Their victim was John Jones, a platelayer on the Shrewsbury and Chester Railway. He had been spending his cash at the Sun Inn, Llangollen, and having drunk a considerable quantity of ale was set upon by George and Mary Jones and another un-named person, who relieved him of 14/-. Though recommended for mercy, they were sent to Van Diemen's Land for seven years.

Little value or use could be given to the pair of boots that Thomas Parry and James Taylor stole from William Sumner of Haighton, Hanmer, but they were stolen, just the same. Both men also helped themselves to clothing and other household goods and both were caught; both were punished with one week's imprisonment and transportation for ten years.

Being a tailor himself, Thomas Slawson knew what to look for in a quality coat, so when he and William Hughes broke into and entered the house of Robert Ethleston, they knew which two coats to take. Thinking they had not been seen, they hid their loot in a hayrick, but were seen, followed, caught and transported for ten years. Slawson, unmarried, had to wait three years for a transport to Western Australia. He was granted a Ticket of Leave on 30 October 1856 and a Certificate of Freedom on 21 September 1863. The rest of his life was spent living in Guilford, Perth, working as a self employed tailor.

William Jones alias William Hardy alias Will Mutton Hall was only a 'small time' member of a gang who were responsible for a great number of petty robberies, sneaking about and breaking into houses and stealing all they could lay their hands on'. That is why he got off fairly lightly with a four-year sentence of transportation on 12 July 1856.

Having the proper tools for the job is most important and that is why Owen Pritchard carried a glazier's diamond in one pocket and a piece of glass in another. Unfortunately for him, they were found after he broke a window at the house of Evan Roberts, Llanarmon yn Iâl. He and his partner Samuel Ryan then entered the house and stole money and other articles. He had £17 (worth £733.72 in 2010), a silver watch and a top coat on him when arrested. He was also found guilty of stealing 8 lbs. of brass and transported for a total of ten years – five for each offence – on 20 March 1861. In his closing speech, the judge described Pritchard as the Welsh 'Jack Sheppard' (a notorious East End villain, who escaped from prison at least six times!) and that he (Pritchard) had escaped from prison twice and had even hidden a homemade rope in the prison toilet in readiness for his third escape attempt!

Edward Davies asked Henry Smith to testify for him in court, but as Smith refused to kiss the Book (Bible) his evidence was not accepted. Both, on 13 July 1861 were sentenced to a period of hard labour at Ruthin Gaol and four and five years respectively in Western Australia because they had broken into and entered the dwelling place of Thomas Williams of Wrexham. They had also stolen twelve knives and forks, a pair of boots and a linen jacket belonging to Job Ward. Their fence (receiver of stolen property), Margaret Davies (probably a relative of Edward) was no help as she was also caught and transported for four years. Smith returned to the Wrexham area where he was put on licence on condition that he reported to the authorities at regular intervals. He did not, and when caught in August 1865, he was convicted for a garden robbery and on 19 February 1865 received the sentenced of three months' hard labour. He was again sentenced at Ruthin Assizes on 20 March 1866 to be transported for eight years for burglary.

Arson is the wilful setting on fire of houses or other property. In a period of eighteen months between August 1863 and March 1865, no less than six people were transported from north Wales for such a crime. A few were reported with very little detail in the Press. Thomas Johnson and James Green, for example, were only given a couple of lines of column space, while William Mason, William Mawson, Ruben Bolton and Thomas Denelope were granted a few more column inches for their crime, which took place in Llantysilio and Wrexham. They were transported for seven years.

Chapter 12

NIMBY (not in my back yard) crimes

In 1784 the journey from London to Holyhead took forty-eight hours on the stage coach. With the building of the A5 and the bridges over the Conwy and the Menai Strait, it could be completed in twenty-seven hours in 1836. By then, travelling had become much more fashionable for the gentry, and was easier even for ordinary folk. Gangs of working navvies travelled the country looking for work and added to the crime statistics. Farm-workers went looking for work during the sheep-shearing period, harvest time etc. so it was not unknown for inhabitants of one county or even strangers to feature in court cases in other parts of Wales.

William Jones was a farmer from Beaumaris, Anglesey who took the long road to Llangrannog in Cardiganshire, where he was caught stealing clothing and a pair of shoes from the premises of Benjamin Owen, a cobbler. On 16 March 1773 William was found guilty of stealing and was sentenced to be transported for seven years.

Another who travelled to Cardiganshire was John Williams, yeoman of Tremeirchion, Flint, who on October 13 1758 was caught in the possession of a horse belonging to Anne Williams, a widow of Llanfihangel Genau'r-glyn. He was sentenced to be transported for fourteen years.

The theft of a horse also features in the case of Thomas Williams, aged fifteen, from Barmouth. His ultimate goal was to get to Liverpool so he stole a horse in Betws Gwerful Goch to help him on his way. Thomas got as far as Wrexham where he was caught: when he tried to sell the horse the law caught up with him. He was originally sentenced to death but, luckily, was pardoned; sentenced to fourteen years transportation, but again pardoned and set free in August 1764.

Another horse thief was Joseph Lee of Amlwch, Anglesey, described as an 'outwasher of brass'. He stole a horse belonging to Edward Roberts, a farmer of St. Asaph. On 12 April 1816, Joseph was sentenced to death, but on consideration, the sentence was changed to one of transportation for life.

Llangian, Caernarvonshire is a small village and quite a distance from Llangristiolus, Anglesey, but John Hughes journeyed all the way from Llangian to Anglesey, stole a heifer and made his way over the Menai Strait, towards England. William Thomas, the rightful owner of the said heifer, would not let the matter rest and pressed for his complaint to be investigated. John, described as a 'desperate character', was caught by the 'Bluemen' in Pwllheli six months later, as he had been working as a drover taking cattle to England. He was sentenced to death on 23 April 1819 but was pardoned by the King and transported for fourteen years. Expenses of £30 were paid by the Court to Thomas Jones, captain of the brig *Esther*, for conveying Hughes to London.

Clynnog Fawr is another small Caernarvonshire village and a place of Christian pilgrimage but Christian principles were not evident in David Roberts' actions. He may well have thought that he had got away with the theft of money from a customer at the Red Lion Inn, Caernarfon, on 28 January 1820; as he laid low for almost a year before venturing as far as Beaumaris on 13 December 1820. There he stole a watch from the house of John Hughes, a shoemaker of the town. His luck didn't hold out; he was caught and tried for both offences and sentenced to be transported for seven years for each offence.

Mary Thomas alias Mary Lewis was either the wife or partner of John Lewis, Holywell, Flint. Her nimble fingers not only made mops, but 'lifted' many a valuable item. She was arrested in her home town and accused of stealing clothes and money belonging to John Jones of Pentraeth, Anglesey. On 2 December 1822 she was sentenced to be transported for seven years.

James Jordan Jones (aged twenty-two) and his younger brother Robert Jordan Jones (aged seventeen) ventured out of the city of Liverpool to Flintshire, where two candlesticks, a hat, a pair of shoes and three books were more than they could resist. On 10 August 1833 they were transported for seven years.

Robert Roberts alias Robin Llys, of Llangernyw, together with Thomas Roberts alias Tom Gors, were both members of what was known as a notorious gang who infested Denbighshire for a length of time stealing horses and sheep etc, and were involved in the theft of a gelding on 27 October 1837 from Edward Birch of Cotton Hall, Denbigh. Their escapades came to an end when caught and tried in March 1838. Tom turned Queen's evidence, not in the hope of a lesser sentence for himself but because Robin had cheated on his partners. Both were sentenced to fifteen years' transportation.

In league together were George Baker, late of Wolverhampton, and Catherine Baker alias Caroline Glover, late of Newcastle, Staffordshire. They shared everything, including the £3 19s. 6d. they stole from William Jones of Bagillt Street, Holywell after they assaulted him and shared the dock in court on 25 March 1848. The jury, 'without hesitation', returned a verdict of guilty and they shared a sentence of transportation for ten years each.

Branded a 'hardened thief' by the court on 25 October 1853, Hugh Morris was on his way 'down under' for ten years after stealing 'wearing apparel' from the *Snowdon Lassie*, a ship docked at harbour at Felinheli. The owner of the clothes must have had quite a shock when he saw them being worn by Hugh and walking towards him on The Maes in Caernarvon! He raised the alarm; Hugh was caught and two previous convictions helped send him on his way.

According to the saying, 'you shouldn't piss in your own

back yard', or you'll only get into trouble. Many dubious characters were willing to risk a spot of law-breaking in someone else's back yard. Unfortunately for them, they were often caught and had to pay the price.

Chapter 13

A matter of luck – some good, some bad

Luck is defined as what chance or fortune sends. It can be said that luck can be good or bad. Some of those unfortunates who were transported could be considered very lucky; others most unlucky, but whatever Lady Luck sends, we have to live with it – but for some convicts it must have been very difficult to live with their bad luck.

According to an old saying, 'We have to live with our family, but can choose our friends'. David Edwards must have rued the fact that one of his family 'grassed' on him.

David, of Dolgellau had stolen a horse on 3 June 1742. At that time, he was employed by Thomas Thomas, a Carmarthen tanner, whose business had 'gone to the wall' but who was friendly with David's cousin – Howell Lewis of Dolgellau. It was this cousin who 'shopped' him, and was responsible for him being sentenced to death originally, but he was reprieved and transported for fourteen years.

One can only sympathise with John Mark, a labourer from the parish of Caernarvon. He was twice indicted for the theft of money and personal goods belonging to a person unknown on 7 December 1753. In court, even the prosecutor's name was unspecified! With no-one to speak against or for him, he was sentenced to be transported for seven years.

Catherine Jones of Caernarvon stole household goods that had had been laid out on a hedge in Bangor to dry on 1 February 1773 – for her, it must have been an opportunity too good to miss – but why did she do it again in May 1773? Why was Jane Owen of Llandwrog tempted to do the same from the same owner of the goods – a man named Richard Fitz, of Llanllechid? Both were transported for seven years.

Another lucky man was William Davies from the parish of Marford and Hosely in Flint. He received stolen property including sugar and rum from John Warburton, cooper; Mark Bage, paper maker; and William Chrimes (an ironic surname), labourer – all of St. Mary upon the Hill, Chester. The three had already been found guilty of theft on 26 December 1778. Davies was indicted with his wife, but had good reason to celebrate the new year as he was found guilty; sentenced to be transported for fourteen years – but eventually granted a free pardon.

Another truly lucky man who was given a free pardon was Edward Rees of Hope, Flintshire. On 11 October 1783 he was reported to have stolen William Edwards' horse, and despite a plea of not guilty, was sentenced to death. He was pardoned and sentenced to transportation for seven years. This was duly commuted to a free pardon.

William Robinson alias Roberts, labourer, from Beaumaris, Anglese, appeared in court on 10 February 1811 charged with stealing clothing from a lodging house where he was staying, which were the property of James Harries, a Beaumaris innkeeper. William was caught in Shrewsbury, following a report about the incident in the *North Wales Gazette*. If he was recognized by someone who had read just a description of him, he could count himself rather unlucky, but an eagle-eyed reader spotted him and he was caught and transported for seven years.

Lewis (alias John) Hughes upset his father-in-law and paid a price. For whatever reason, Lewis' father-in-law was upset, so he 'shopped' his son-in-law for being a bigamist. Lewis had married, firstly, Margaret Hughes of Holywell, Flintshire on 5 July 1806 and secondly, Eleanor Edwards of Corwen on 8 June 181. He had seven years in Australia to consider his actions.

Today, it may well be 'politically incorrect' to call someone 'stupid' but it is a fitting adjective for a bigamist who upsets his father-in-law. It also befits someone who, already serving a sentence in Caernarfon Gaol, steals the lead off the roof. Such a man was William Roberts, who was transported for the offence in 1817.

Some accept their luck; others seem to chance their luck. Evan Evans of Llandderfel, Meirionethshire must have been a chancer. On 7 September 1818 he stole a sheep, the property of Edward Davies, a farmer. He then fled the scene of crime and might have got away only he chanced his luck and tried to sell the same sheep to the innkeeper of Druid Inn, Gwyddelwern. For both his crimes – stealing and selling stolen property – he was sentenced to death, pardoned and transported for seven years.

Another who fled the S.O.C. (scene of crime) was Moses Rowland of Hope, Flint, but for Moses it was a matter of jumping from the frying pan into the fire. A youngster of only fifteen years, he made his way with stolen money and silver watches from Hope to his sister's house at Hulme, Lancashire. Unfortunately for him, his elder brother was more of a law-abiding citizen and it was he who 'shopped' Moses to the authorities, from whom he received a sentence of death. Pardoned, like many others, he was transported for seven years.

Another very lucky man was John Williams, who stole a sheep, the property of Thomas Williams, Glan y Bala, Llanddeiniolen. He was found with the carcass and had a knife in his hand at Fachwen Quarry, Deiniolen. The sentence of the court on 22 March 1834 was that he be transported for life – and that is what would have happened were it not for the fact that an amazing twenty-two of his friends appeared in court as character witnesses. The *Caernarvon Herald* does not state his reasons for committing such a crime, but his family would surely have blessed his share of luck in having such fine friends.

In the case of Charles Foulkes of Wrexham, it is difficult to work out whether it was bad luck or bad judgement on the part of his mother that had him transported for ten years. He had stolen a pewter pint measure from the Crown Inn, Aber Street, Wrexham, taken it home and hidden it under his bed. He must have shown it to his mother because when the police came looking for him, his mother denied he was home but was later heard to say, 'Charley, there are two policemen in the house that want you and about a pewter pot'. With no means of escape, poor Charley took the pot from under his bed and threw it out of the window into the street! He made his eighth court appearance on 23 March 1844 to be told of his sentence.

Being sentenced to be transported to Australia may well have been a fate almost worse than death for many. What probably hurt more than anything was facing the reality that it meant never being able to return home, however much a reformed character they became – and to give them their due, many did reform and turn out to be model citizens.

Reported in the *Caernarvon and Denbigh Herald* on 31 March 1849 was the case of John Williams and Daniel Jones who pleaded guilty to a series of six indictments of a burglary and five larcenies! As the properties were scattered over Anglesey and the offences ranged over a period of time, the judge was convinced that the prisoners were 'systematic thieves.' Yet, they had the cool impudence to call witnesses to character, one of whom said that if he were to speak the truth on oath, he could not commend them. After suitable reproach for their thieving, a sentence of one week's hard labour was passed for each offence and transportation for seven years for breaking and entering the house of Robert Roberts of Holyhead.

Despite tough restrictions, a few did manage to make their way back home after transportation. One can only imagine how they felt on seeing the coast of Wales once again, or how they felt on returning to their homes and loved ones. They were, probably, more than ready to keep on the straight and narrow and lie low. But William Williams was different. He was one of those known as a 'Ticket of Leave' man. He had, somehow, successfully returned to Anglesey, where he could have enjoyed his remaining years with his family, free from worries and far away from the harsh Australian life.

This William could well be the same Llangadwaladr man who had been transported for ten years in 1840. He was originally sentenced to be transported for life, but the term was later reduced to one of ten years. If he is the same one, his period of ten years would long have come to an end by 1856. In March of that year William Williams, by then of Brynsiencyn (not that far from Llangadwaladr), appeared in court on a charge of stealing a pair of boots and a pair of stockings on 2 January 1856 from a house in Brynsiencyn. A case against William being found guilty was based on the fact that he had not actually *broken into* the house in question – as he was staying there. It was his mother's house, where she cohabited with a man she was intending to marry. William apparently didn't like his future stepfather, and on his way out of the house one morning took the boots and stockings and threw them over a hedge. He was found guilty and because of a previous conviction was given another sentence of ten years' transportation.

Chapter 14

'He that ruleth over men must be just.'
(Samuel, Chapter 23, verse 3)

Before any Assize court sat, the judge would proceed to the local church to listen to a sermon: 'On the following day (Sunday) his lordship attended divine service in the chapel of St. Mary, where an appropriate sermon was preached by the Rev. Hugh Jones of Llanfaes, the Sheriff's Chaplain, from Romans Ch.4 v10.' (Beaumaris, October 1842).

Whether listening to the sermon had any effect on the judge's conscience is debatable. He was in Beaumaris to apply a law which, at times, was extremely harsh. To give judges and lawyers of the day their due, however, some cases were directed to be found Not Guilty when it was quite obvious that the prisoner in the dock was the perpetrator of the crime in question.

But is has to be asked whether some of these judges were the most suitable people to judge their fellow men. For example, take the case of Anne Williams alias Edwards of Llanfechell, Anglesey, in 1842 (See Chapters 1 and 7 above) the grand jury consisted of members of the county's gentry and ruling class, whose lives were far removed from that of a poor mill carrier's daughter. Among those present were:

- Hon. Charles C. Vivian, MP, Foreman.
- The Honourable William Owen Stanley, MP (1802–1884). Born in Alderley, Cheshire, he was twin brother to the Second Baron Stanley of Alderley. He was a noted solicitor and spent much of his time on his estates outside Anglesey.

He was a firm believer in social and religious freedom and argued strongly against the unification of the Bangor and St. Asaph diocese.

- William Bulkeley Hughes, Esquire, MP (1797–1882). Born in Plas Coch and could trace his family back to Llywarch ap Bran. He was educated at Harrow School and was Member of Parliament for the Caernarfon Boroughs. As a land owner he had 4,697 acres to his name. He was also chairman of the Anglesey Central Railway Company.

- Richard T. Griffith, Esq. Bodwyr Isaf. High Sheriff of Anglesey in 1850. Owned 4,873 acres of land.

- Vice Admiral Robert Lloyd, Plas Tregaean (born 24 March 1765): a noted sailor who served his country in many battles and as captain of such ships as *Hussar, Plantagenet, Mars, Valiant, Latona* (a thirty-eight gun ship), *Hebe, Robust, Racoon* and the *Swiftsure*. He was refused permission by a judge to join the *Hussar* on March 29 1807 as he was a member of the jury at the Beaumaris Courthouse. After retiring from the *Swiftsure* he came home to enjoy a rich and varied social life especially as a member of the Beaumaris Book Society, which he founded, and later renamed as the Royal Anglesey Yacht Club.

- John Williams, Esq.: successful businessman and the owner of an Amlwch Port shipyard. He died in 1851.

- Stephen Roose, Esq., Glan y Don: an immigrant to Anglesey who worked as an agent in Parys Mountain.

- John Paynter, Esq., Maes y Llwyn: land owner and corn merchant. A Justice of the Peace and was appointed High Sheriff for the county in 1871.

- Rice Roberts, Esq., Plas Llangefni & Treffos (1784–8 July 1876): educated at Eton and Oxford. He lived in Chester and was elected mayor of the city three times. Even so, he was also active in Anglesey's social life and was chairman of the Quarter Sessions for fifty-two years.

- Henry Webster, Esq., whose house was named 'Vitriol' (a

type of oil produced at Parys Mountain by pouring water on scrap metal).

- James Treweek: given the title of 'Captain', which reflected his social status when he lived and worked in Cornwall and was the owner of a tin mine. He came to Amlwch in October 1811 as manager of the Mona Mine Company. He became a very successful businessman and was the owner of an Amlwch Port shipyard. He died in 1851.

'They are like two nations that have no contact or sympathy. They know little of each other's habits, thoughts and feelings...' That is how Benjamin Disraeli described the two very differing strata of society – the Poor and the Rich. It was, in reality, a simple division. If you were poor, life was always hard, but if you were lucky enough to be one of the rich, life was much easier in that clothes, food and a roof over their heads were much more easily come by for them than for poor people.

At times, the presiding Lord Chief Justice, would do the rounds of the north Wales Assizes. Thomas Denman was born in London and educated at Eton and St. John's College, Cambridge. He was called to the Bar in 1806 and quickly made a name for himself in the defence of the Luddites and as counsel for Queen Caroline – which made him the King's enemy. He was twice elected as a Whig MP; once for Wareham and once for Nottingham. In 1830 he became Attorney General; in 1832 Lord Chief Justice and was made a peer in 1834.

Sir Thomas Noon Talfourd (26 May 1795 to 13 March 1854) was well known as a judge and author. He was the son of a wealthy brewer in Reading, Berkshire. He was educated at Hendon and Reading Grammar School before going to London to study law under Joseph Chitty. Called to the Bar in 1820 he became a judge in Oxford in 1821. Later, he was appointed judge of the Court of Common Pleas. In 1835, he was elected MP for Reading. He had friends in literary circles and Charles Dickens dedicated *The Pickwick Papers* to him. Talfourd himself was also an author, a playwright and a poet of some repute. His death occurred in court at Stafford. Dickens was one of the mourners at his funeral at West Norwood Cemetery.

The first Baron Abinger, James Scarlett Abinger, was born in Jamaica. In 1785, he was sent to London to further his education and went to Trinity College, Cambridge. He graduated in 1789 and after entering the Inner Temple, he was called to the bar in 1791. Afterwards he joined the northern circuit and the Lancashire sessions. After taking silk in 1816, he became the most successful lawyer at the bar. As a Whig, he first entered parliament as member for Peterborough in 1819. In 1830, he defected to the Tories and was elected member for Colchester, then Norwich in 1832. He died at his lodgings, whilst on the Norfolk circuit on 7 April 1844. However brilliant a lawyer he was reputed to have been, he was also described as being partial, dictatorial, vain and domineering in his attitude towards juries.

Another baron who found himself on the north Wales circuit was John Campbell. Born in 1779 he was educated at the United College, St. Andrews. He took silk in 1827; became a member of parliament for Stafford in 1830. Amongst the most famous cases that he appeared in as a lawyer was the prosecution of John Frost, Chartist leader. When he was appointed Chief Justice of the Queen's bench, he was criticized for attempting to influence juries. In 1859 he was made Lord Chancellor but his time in office was undistinguished. He died in 1861.

At least one judge on the north Wales circuit was known as a practical and knowledgeable one with a fine judicial sense of humour. William Henry Maule was born in 1788 in Edmonton, Middlesex. Privately educated, then at Trinity College, Cambridge, he became interested in Mathematics due to his friendship with Charles Babbage, a mathematician and founder member of the Astronomical Society in 1820. Maule was offered the post of Professor of Mathematics at the East India College, but he had entered Lincoln's Inn in 1810 with the intention of practising law. He was called to the bar in 1814. Due to ill health, he retired from the bench in 1855 and died three years later.

One of Maule's students, when he was a mathematics tutor, was Cresswell Cresswell. A descendant of a Northumberland family, Cresswell Cresswell was born in 1794. Educated at Charterhouse and Emmanuel College, Cambridge he studied at the Middle Temple and was called to the bar in 1819. Having joined the northern circuit he earned a distinguished reputation amongst other lawyers and judges. In 1842, he was made a judge and knighted at the same time. A fall from his horse led to his death on 29 July 1863.

Sir William Bovill (26 May 1814 to 1 November 1873), English judge, was born at Allhallows, Barking. After leaving school, he was articled to a firm of solicitors. He was called to the bar in 1841 and joined the home circuit. His special training in a solicitor's office, and its resulting connection, combined with a thorough knowledge of the details of engineering, acquired through his interest in a manufacturing firm in the east end of London, soon brought him a very extensive patent and commercial practice. He became Queen's Counsel in 1855, and on 28 March 1857 was elected Member of Parliament for Guildford. In the House of Commons he was very keen for legal reform, and the Partnership Law Amendment Act 1865, which he helped to pass, is always referred to as Bovill's Act. In 1866 he was appointed Solicitor General, an office which he left when he became Chief Justice of the Common Pleas in November of the same year. He died at Kingston upon Thames, on the 1 November 1873. His great patience and courtesy gained him the respect and affection of the fellow members of his profession.

Other judges and chairmen of the bench, who may have had a little more knowledge of north Wales were:
• Henry Cecil Raikes – the son of the chancellor of the diocese of Chester, he married into a Welsh family – Charlotte Blanche Trevor-Roper of Plas Teg, Mold. As well as being prominent in legal circles, he was also a politician and was

Conservative MP for Chester (1868–1880), Preston (1882) and Cambridge University (1882–1891).He was also one of the earliest politicians to have his voice recorded for Thomas Edison. To his credit, he also lived in north Wales, which obviously gave him a better insight into the lives of the people who stood before him in court. It was at Llwynegrin Hall that he died on 24 August 1891.

- Sir Love Parry Jones-Parry (1772–1843) of the Jones-Parry family, inherited the Madryn estate and lived there whilst chairman of the Caernarvon bench. The family held lands in Caernarvonshire and Denbighshire. As a young man, he served in the Army and spent time in America. He was an MP, firstly for Horsham and afterwards for the Caernarvon Boroughs. Noted as a philanthropist, his generosity was 'proverbial' and his reputation gained him the name of 'the poor man's friend'.

- Lloyd Kenyon was decended from a Welsh family on his mother's side and was born in Gredington, Flintshire on 1 April 1805. He was educated at Harrow and Christ Church, Oxford. He was Tory MP for St. Michael's, Cornwall (1830–1832) but failed to be elected MP for Denbighshire in 1833. In the same year he married Georgina de Gray by whom he had 10 children – 5 sons, 5 daughters. His death occurred at Eastbourne on 24 July 1864. Family connections with Flintshire meant that he asked to be buried at Hanmer, Flintshire.

In their red or black robes, judges presided over the courts of north Wales from their elevated chairs or bench. In the eighteenth and nineteenth centuries, another part of their standard uniform was a long wig which could well have frightened or intimidated many who stood before them. Some – for reasons already stated – may not have fully understood the relevance of what the judge had to say, but the judges' reactions to their cases certainly affected their future.

Chapter 15

Under the magnifying glass

Some of the cases reported above made little impression – perhaps only a few details were included in the press reports or maybe they were so similar to many others.

Other stories were read many times over because they gave a clear insight of life as it was at the time, or because a degree of compassion and sympathy was felt with those in the dock. In some cases, further research led to gleaning some of the life history of the accused and how they, later, lived their lives, in some cases very successfully, in Australia or New Zealand. In a few cases, one can only admire the impudence of the main characters.

The stories in this chapter are worthy of a little more attention to detail as they represent a cross-section of all the cases represented in this book.

CASE NUMBER 1
Jessie White made a niche for herself in Anglesey's history in 1849. She was a member of a gang which included: Thomas Taylor, William White, James Emanuel Crabb, James Brown, William Watkins and George Hand – all of whom were transported. When caught, one gang member pleaded his innocence before the court but was none the wiser, despite his disabilities. Their crime was house-breaking. Some members had been stealing before. Thomas Taylor had been before the court accused of stealing items of leather from Hugh Ellis. Taylor, William White and an accomplice named John Brewer had been accused of stealing shoes, laths and leather, the

property of John Williams. Taylor and William White were found not guilty, but Brewer was not cleared. All gang members were found guilty of housebreaking and stealing property belonging to John Hughes, cobbler/shoe maker, Hen Bandy (Old Woollen Factory), Bodedern. According to newspaper reports, Sir Richard Williams Bulkeley said in court that it was shocking to see the prisoners, all young Englishmen [*sic*] between the ages of seventeen and twenty-five years, who had gone into the island with others still at large, with no other object than to commit depredations.

Anglesey Quarter Sessions

These sessions were held in the County Hall, Beaumaris on Tuesday and Wednesday last. Magistrates present were Sir R. B. Williams Bulkeley, Bart, MP, Chairman; Rt. Hon. Lord Vivian; Lloyd J. Price, Esq.; Stephen Roose, Esq., High Sheriff; Rev. O.G. Williams; N.M. Goddard, Esq.; Hugh Beaver, Esq.

William White, Thomas Taylor, James Emmanuel Crabb, James Brown, William Watkins, George Harris and a female called Jessie White were indicted for having broken into the house of John Hughes, shoe maker, living at Hen Bandy, near Bodedern, on the 24th of November last, and stealing therefrom a variety of wearing apparel, eight and a half sovereigns and a variety of other articles.

They were also charged for a second count, with feloniously receiving the property, knowing it to have been stolen.

John Hughes . . . deported . . . that on the night of the 23rd November last he retired with his family about 10 o'clock after fastening the door and seeing the windows were secured . . . He arose at 5 o'clock on the morning of 24th. November and the door of his house was ajar, and a pane of glass in the window broken, the fastening removed...went to Llangefni and Beaumaris and saw several items of clothing which he identified as his property.

James Emmanuel Crabb whose sight was stated to have

been injured by the bursting of a steam engine appealed to the jury for an acquittal on the grounds of the improbability of his being present at the robbery, when it was known that he was obliged to be led in the night...

Sir Richard Williams Bulkeley said that the evidence upon which the prisoners were convicted was so satisfactory that no doubt could remain of their guilt. It was certain that they were part of a gang of vagabonds who had come into the island for no other purpose than top commit depredations...

The infirmity spoken of by Crabb was no excuse for him nor could it make any difference to the punishment...

Thomas Taylor had also been charged of stealing etc. in the village of Llanbedrgoch.

(*Caernarvon and Denbigh Herald*, January 5 1850.)

A sentence of transportation for 10 years was passed upon them. Watkins, an unmarried labourer, was sent out to Freemantle on the *Sea Park*. He was granted a Ticket of Leave on April 5 1854 and is known to have worked as a self employed carpenter in 1854. William White, originally from Glasgow, also travelled on the same ship and was granted a Ticket of Leave on the same date.

The only female in the gang – Jessie Wheeler, nee White – was born in 1832 in Airdrie, Scotland. She was transported for a period of ten years following her arrest and conviction at the Quarter Sessions in Beaumaris. As a member of a travelling gang, she followed village fairs and this is what brought her and her companions to Bodedern. While many houses in the village were empty whilst their occupants were at the fair, the gang would carry out a robbery. Jessie, at sixteen years of age and just under five foot in height, might well have been the one to gain admittance for this gang. Another member had the same surname as her but it is not known if they were brother and sister or father and daughter? If that is unclear, the facts that are available give a pretty comprehensive picture of her life before and after transportation.

Awaiting her transfer from Beaumaris Gaol to London, Jessie did not curry favour with the Matron. The punishment book of Beaumaris Gaol for 1850 shows that she was punished on March 16 for 'Singing and Shouting in her bedroom and being insolent to the Matron'. She was put in solitary confinement and on a bread and water diet for two days.

On 7 March 1851, the *Emma Eugenia* arrived at Hobart, Van Diemen's Land. On board was Jessie. Eleven months later, she gave birth to a son (d.o.b 12 February 1852), whom she named William (same name as his father/grandfather/uncle.) This child could have been the result of a liaison or rape: the rape of women convicts was common, as they were considered the same as prostitutes and the British authorities deliberately sent out young women for this very purpose.

On 29 March 1853, Jessie was considered for a Conditional Pardon, which was approved on 20 May 1856. She had also been granted permission to marry on 22 October 1855 the free settler (one who had travelled to Australia of his own accord) William Wheeler. William was born in Berkshire circa 1813. He was transported to Tasmania aboard the *John Calvin* (a Greenock-built bark of 510 tons) leaving Woolwich on 7 January 1846, and travelling via Tenerife. The ship arrived on Norfolk Island on 21 September. The voyage took 129 days. A hundred and ninety five prisoners were landed at Norfolk Island, regarded by many as a 'living hell'.

The marriage ceremony took place at the Anglican Church of St. George, Hobart. Once her sentence was completed, the family, which now included two daughters, Mary (d.o.b. 1 July 1858; died in Tasmania 1860) and Hannah (d.o.b. 11 September 1860), left for Dunedin, New Zealand, where William continued to work as a labourer.

Jessie Wheeler, reformed character, died of enteritis and congestion of the lungs on 26 November 1901 at Frederick Street, Dunedin and was buried with her husband in the Northern Cemetery, Dunedin.

(Her father is, confusingly, recorded on her death certificate as William Hamilton. This might be a mistake as Hamilton is a place near Airdrie. But was her maiden name Hamilton? What was her relationship to the other gang member – William White? Was she born in Hamilton or Airdrie? They are within walking distance of each other and about nine miles from Glasgow city centre. Family members in New Zealand are still trying to find the answers.)

Amongst the seven other burials recorded for the same plot are: William Wheeler (husband) died of pneumonia in 1882, and Dorothea (Dora) Ford Gillies Wheeler, fourth child of Jessie and William Wheeler; died 1894.

On a document showing returns of the Freeholders of New Zealand, dated 1882 (the year of her husband's death), Jessie is recorded as having an estate worth £200 in the borough of North East Valley, Dunedin, and on the 1893 Dunedin Electoral Roll her occupation is given as a 'storekeeper with residential property in Frederick Street and Athol Place, Dunedin'. She was, by then, a pillar of the community.

Another child of the marriage was John Wheeler, born circa 1860. His age on his February 15 1884 marriage certificate granted in Dunedin, New Zealand is given as twenty-four years of age; his birthplace as Tasmania. On the certificate, his mother's surname is given as Hamilton, possibly an attempt to cover his mother's dubious past, according to his great-grandchild. At the time of his marriage his occupation was a 'hawker' – one who travels selling wares, a pedlar, a packman. He married Isabella Crawford Gillies. Her parents were Daniel Gillies and Mary Stewart (reputed to have been related to the Royal Stewarts), who emigrated from Rothesay on the Isle of Bute in 1859. Later he drove a horse-drawn cab, then a tram. Twice he was declared bankrupt. He also had medical problems i.e. diabetes. John died on 5 December 1910 and is buried in Dunedin's Northern Cemetery.

Also buried with him are his wife and an unmarried

daughter, Madgie. Another child died whilst she was ten years old – Alma Isabella Wheeler. The cemetery is now closed, but many of Dunedin's earliest citizens are buried there.

CASE NUMBER 2

At one time, the United Kingdom was mostly wooded and all the forests and rivers were for everyone's use. After 1066, the manorial system was introduced by which common land and common rights have their origins. The Lord of the Manor was granted land by the King and his estate (or 'manor') became the foundation on which a rural economy was built. Under the feudal system, the ones who toiled the land were under the protection of said Lord in return for their labours. After gathering the harvests from the manor's land, the open field strips and hay meadows were made available for common grazing. Over the years, more and more common land was fenced off or enclosed for private use. The removal of common access rights to the land by the Enclosures Acts led to hundreds dying of starvation whilst others were forced to move to towns and cities to live and earn their living. Between 1767 and 1867 seven million acres of common land were fenced in. Part of this land included the common land at the foot of Yr Eifl, on the Llŷn peninsula, Gwynedd.

Robert William Hughes was a victim of the enclosure of this common land. Official documents have précised his story into a few lines such as:

Accused: Robert Will Hughes; Parish: Pistyll;
        County: Caernarvon;
Status: Labourer;
Offence: Enclosure Riot . . . Verdict: Guilty;
Punishment: Death, pardoned, transported for life.

However, his life story deserves a better telling than that. He was only a poor cottager, who tended his smallholding on the slopes of Yr Eifl, but he posed a threat to Richard Ellis, gent. and so was forcibly removed.

Towards the end of the eighteenth century about a quarter of the land area of Wales was considered to be common land on which animals were grazed, crops grown, minerals mined or quarried. By the second half of the nineteenth century almost a fifth, or a million acres, of this common land had been enclosed. People who lived on the land (or 'squatters' as they were considered) had to move losing all their rights. Had they lived in their stone houses for a period of more than forty years, they were exempt from moving. Local gentry, through their land agents and stewards, laid claim to much of the land, sometimes without notice to others, but Robert William Hughes had other ideas. He was not about to be moved and on a given signal by him on a conch shell, up to eighty of his neighbours joined him in resisting the Dragoons who had been moved into the area to shift Robert and his ilk out of their homes.

A local concession was that those who had built their own cottages in one night and had been living in them for twenty years were allowed to stay. Everyone else had to leave – otherwise they were prosecuted. Robert did not fit neatly into any category and was caught by the Militia and charged with being 'Captain of the Mob'.

Despite his plea of not guilty, he was found guilty and sentenced to death for his part in a riot.

The prisoner having received His Majesty's pardon, on being transported for Life, I do humbly order you to make the usual order for transporting him, and for authorising the Magistrates of the said county to contract for removing him on board one of the hulks for prisoners under sentence for transportation according to the directions of the Secretary of State.

(Lord Justice Temple. 26 June 1813)

His removal to London from the county gaol at Caernarfon necessitated a great deal of work for his keeper William Griffith.

Paid at Caernarfon	12s 0d
Boat to go on board	3s 0d
To Woolwich	7s 0d
Woolwich to London	8s 0d
Paid for victuals for 4 persons 4 days	£4 0s 0d
Lodgings at London	0s 0d
Coachman	10s 0d
Guard	10s 0d
Coming home from London to Corwen	£4 14s 0d
To Capel Curig	12s 0d
Coachman to Caernarfon	10s 0d
Meat and Drink	£3 0s 0d
For the journey of the gaoler and his daughter to guard the prisoners, – absent 8 days, and for his son's wages for attending the gaol in his absence	£10 0s 0d
	June 26th 1813.

On 28 July 1813 he was placed, with another twenty-three convicts, aboard the *General Hewart*, moored at Woolwich on the Thames. Many of his fellow travellers were sickly and emaciated, and the majority suffered from scurvy or typhus. The ship sailed to Madeira (nine days out of Portsmouth) and by the time it had reached Rio de Janeiro (eighty-three days out of Portsmouth) had been sailing through almost continual tropical rain. Nineteen people had died and many more were ill because their bedding had been thrown overboard, waterlogged; when a cold spell of weather appeared many could not survive the cold. By then dysentery had also broken out on board and no-one, at the time, realised how contagious it was. Before arriving at Port Jackson, Sydney, thirty-four people had been buried at sea.

The ship's record includes:

> Hughes, Robert William. Gen Hewitt. Carnarvory.
> 5 April 1813 . . . Life . . .
> Labourer . . . very old and feeble.

On arrival, Robert was immediately transferred to Rooty Hill Hospital where he and another 49 convicts were set to work as labourers. An extra detail in his records mentions that he was unmarried and had not written his will. He died on Tuesday, 21 August 1832, King William IV's anniversary. Due to the importance of the date, his name is not recorded – just that he died in the Hospital on a day regarded as a holiday and that he was interred with another un-named convict who died the previous day. They were not offered privacy, even in death!

Today the hospital has been turned into a church and its records include:

> 1831. No. 41. Robert Hughes, of Port Maquarie, buried August 21st, aged 70, by the Rev. John Cross.

It is known that Mrs. Cross was from mid Wales, but there are no records of her indulging any of the convicts with a conversation in Welsh.

Sadly, Robert had no descendants and he may well have been utterly forgotten by now had it not been for Ioan Mai, a local historian, who put his story to paper. (*O Ben Llŷn i Botany Bay*, Gwasg Carreg Gwalch 1993.)

CASE NUMBER 3

'Death', 'pardoned', 'transported for life' are words and phrases which make grim reading. Hearing of such a sentence for a crime committed in their locality must have sent shivers down the spine of the inhabitants of Llandderfel, a quiet village in Merionethshire. They may also have had sympathy for the vicar, since it was at his house that a burglary occurred on 23 May 1813.

Servants at Palé, the clergyman's residence, had quite a shock when they got up on the morning in question. They found that burglars had been in the kitchen and raided the pantry. A piece of cold beef, a piece of ham and part of a cold roast fillet of veal were missing, together with a pocket pistol from another part of the house. Rev. Mr. John Lloyd, his staff and fellow villagers started a search for the culprit(s). An unnamed person said he had seen a suspicious-looking character proceeding in the direction of Corwen and that he had been seen at Llandrillo on his way through. The burglar was captured and identified as Daniel Jones of Llandderfel. The stolen meat was found on him, wrapped up in a handkerchief. Had it been only one piece of meat, he might have got away with his crime as it would have been difficult to identify, but when he was found to have an assortment of meats, there was no arguing. He was also found to be carrying a butcher's knife and a pair of scissors which were produced in court as evidence of the prisoner's crime. The jury had no hesitation in finding him guilty and sentenced him on the strength of evidence placed before them, i.e. the meat, and testimony given in court.

CASE NUMBER 4

George alias William Thomas Smith was a man fleet of foot and had a good working knowledge of north and south Wales. He had a previous conviction against him in Carmarthenshire. George Steven, on oath, swore that George Flynn and William Thomas Smith were one and the same man who, after being caught housebreaking in Carmarthenshire, had been transported for seven years. He (GS) had the certificate to prove it and was adamant that he (GF) did not deserve a second chance. We know not what it was that brought Flynn home from Australia nor why he was in Flintshire on 19 November 1856 but he was charged with breaking into the house of Mary

Williams and stealing a quantity of wearing apparel, the property of John Lloyd.

Mr. V. Williams, lawyer for the prosecutor, called John Lloyd to the witness box. John stated that he was a lodger at the house in question. On the day the offence took place, he had gone to work as usual. When he returned for his dinner, he found the door locked and the key in the usual hiding place. On unlocking the door and entering the house, he spotted a broken window large enough for a man to gain entry. His clothes were gone! Some articles of clothing were shown to him which he identified as his own. The prisoner, rather impudently, cross-examined the witness, but was unable to shake his testimony.

Next to be called was John Jones, a publican of Llanfyllin, who remembered the prisoner coming to his house and offering a coat for sale which he bought for 10/-. Jones, reluctantly, had to give the coat as evidence to David Davies, policeman. There was no sign of a stolen pair of trousers.

Mary Williams was called and stated that she remembered locking the front door on the night of the robbery and also seeing the clothes which belonged to her two sons. PC Jones said he found the prisoner wearing a coat, waistcoat and trousers when apprehended, which he believed to be the stolen property.

'The prisoner addressed the jury in his own defence at some length but very little to his advantage. He called no witnesses. The judge summed up with care, found him guilty, and sentenced him to be transported for six years. 'The prisoner said he had not had a fair trial. (laughter in court.)' He had the good grace to remain quiet afterwards – unlike one prisoner at another hearing who threatened to bring back a ring-tailed monkey as a present for the judge!

CASE NUMBER 5

A written description can often be misleading, as is proved in the case of Hannah Roberts of Holywell, Flint. In the July 1842 press, she is described as 'a short, hazel eyed, round faced girl; a housemaid, industrious, honest with no previous convictions.' Just the type to make someone a very good wife probably – but Hannah was already married, engaged in an affair with John Parry, and expecting his child.

John Parry of Pandy, Caerwys wanted to be rid of Hannah's husband. Full of ideas but not able to carry them out, he persuaded his mistress to sort out the matter of the cuckolded husband. This she did, by putting a dose of poison in his food – which the poor man promptly ate. He lingered for a week before dying a horrible death.

Hannah was aged nineteen. Her husband Robert Roberts was aged seventy-five! They lived near Holywell Racecourse after marrying in May 1841. Before dying, Robert was reported to have said that he had eaten his supper, lobscouse, and that it was about nine or ten o'clock. After which he was sick but recovered. He added that on the previous Monday he had taken some gruel which was made by his wife. He then went out, and threw up a large quantity in the yard close to the house door, which was immediately eaten up by the sow. Maybe he suspected his wife of being unfaithful, as he said that she had been in the habit of walking on the common until eleven or twelve o'clock at night.

When Robert passed away, the doctor who was called said he suspected arsenic poisoning. John Craft Roberts, recalled that Hannah had gone to the surgery to ask for poison for herself, and saying that she was in the family way by another man. On asked about her part in her husband's death, she confessed. A constable was called. Further evidence showed that Hannah had been to the druggist shop, asking for 1d. worth of arsenic. John Bancroft, chemist on duty, said he could only supply 2d. worth, which he sold to her – after labelling the bottle clearly with the word ARSENIC. She called again, asking for a dose of castor oil for the sow; a dose of Epsom Salts and 1d. worth of magnesia. On this visit, she asked the chemist to lie for her should anyone ask what she bought and why. She even offered him a bribe! As well as describing the symptoms of her husband's final, fatal illness, she also said that he had changed his will and that she was no longer the chief beneficiary. Hannah also denied that she had poisoned the lobscouse and that she had used the arsenic to kill rats. After emptying the bottle, she washed it with water, with which she made a cake – which was later eaten by the unfortunate Robert.

When Hannah was allowed to speak to the court, she said that it was John who persuaded her to marry Robert, buy the poison, and be rid of him. If Robert were to die, John would then marry her and enjoy their ill-gotten gains from the deceased's will.

Robert died at 5 a.m. on Monday, 20 June 1842. John slipped away quietly, but Hannah was to appear at another hearing which was reported on 6 August 1842. She called Elizabeth Griffith as a witness, who said that Hannah took her to the chemist shop, where she saw a white powder on the counter, but she didn't know what it was. Hannah said it was for a pain in her breast. She was also told to deny any knowledge of the poison. By then, the sow was reported to have become very ill; Robert had changed his will and his son was told by his father that he knew he had been poisoned.

Whilst in gaol, a piece of paper was found in Hannah's possession which was a copy of the first will which gave her all the household furniture, cattle, heifer, six sheep and lambs, one ass. There was also a codicil which gave his son and daughter a shilling each to be paid immediately. All this she would lose if found guilty.

A Mr. Townsend spoke for Hannah 'with great energy and effect for nearly an hour', drawing attention to her youth, ignorance and credulity. Whilst Robert Roberts was 'of patriarchal age; she was a mere girl'. The jury retired for an hour and a half and returned a verdict of guilty but recommended her to mercy. The prisoner received the sentence with great indifference, in fact she seemed not to understand its purport. The Judge then put on the Black Cap', and she was sentenced to death.

Mr. Townsend, again on Hannah's behalf, pleaded pregnancy and that she was quick with child which was reason enough to be a bar of execution. A jury of matrons confirmed this and 'execution was respited.' Hannah was sentenced to be transported for life to Van Diemen's Land. She sailed on the *Emma Eugenia* in 1844. The ship's records describe her as being of 'a giddy disposition, poor but respectable'.

By 1846, she found herself a new husband – John Cadby – and was reported to be living quietly. By 1850, John had disappeared and Hannah was caught out after hours in a public house for which she was punished with a month's hard labour and not allowed to work in Hobart.

She found herself another man by 1852, whom she claimed to be her husband. For this crime (probably designated 'prostitution') she was punished with another month's hard labour. Later she was found with 'a male prisoner of the crown concealed in a bedroom for an improper purpose', for which she had to spend thirty days in a cell. She repeated the offence a month later and was given three months hard labour. She was granted a Ticket of Leave in 1854 and 'lived a life of drink and men'.

Afterthoughts

In the early years of the twenty-first century, we can look back at the system of transportation and one can only be thankful that it is now a designated part of History. But it cannot be ignored. Facts cannot be altered.

Some, it has to be said, were in favour of transportation. For the government of the day it was a cheaper method of dealing with prisoners in gaols. George Bernard Shaw said that the problems of all countries could be solved by 'extirpating the inhabitants.' An opinion voiced in *The Quarterly Review* of 1828 suggested that the 'entire removal of the individual to a new scene of life affords at once the only security to society against his future crimes . . . '

A letter sent to William Cox was quoted in *The Cambrian* (Swansea) on June 10 1840:

'When you reflect that convicts are chiefly made up of the scum of the earth, ought it not to be a matter of surprise that they are so *well* conducted?'

Another letter appeared in the *Caernarvon and Denbigh Herald* of June 5 1847 which had been sent by a Mr. Jones of Glanbeuno near Caernarvon. It says that transportation brought convicts 'into a very good state of discipline'.

Others were against the system. The philosopher Jeremy Bentham had been opposed to it from the very beginning, and in the 1790s quoted amongst his objections the cost, the uncertainty of the punishment, the fact that there would be few to supervise the convicts in Australia and the lack of evidence of the reformation of the ones sent out there. Another objecter was William Wilberforce, who saw transportation as being very much like slavery.

In 1813, the *Edinburgh Review* contained a paragraph which condemned transportation, 'the miserable wretch, after rotting in a hulk for a year or two . . . is conveyed to a life of alternating slavery and rebellion . . .' Sir William Molesworth was an MP who opposed the system of transportation and in April 1837 helped establish a select committiee in the House of Commons to '...inquire into the system of Transportation, its Efficacy as a Punishment, its influence on the Moral State of Society in the penal Colonies, and how far it is susceptible of improvement.' The committee's first report proposed that transportation be ended as soon as possible.

A letter published in *The Cambrian* on 29 July 1843 (author unknown) described conditions for prisoners as akin to slavery, and convict life in New South Wales as the most dreary and miserable that could be imagined.Life was likened to a lingering death. 'Were those who commit crimes in this country aware of the hardships and privations in the penal colonies, they would sooner perish in their own country, then [sic] render themselves liable to be transported as a felon, to linger out the deeply miserable life of a convict in New South Wales.'

Feelings ran so high that letters from Australian newspapers were copied and printed in English editions to convey the strength of feelings and arguments against transportation. One such letter appeared in the *Cornwall Chronicle* on 26 May 1852. It had originally been sent to the *Hobart Town Advertiser* under the heading of 'Prisoner servants and their employers':

'the following is related to the treatment of a servant of this class received from her mistress; it seems to argue the probability, if not certainty, that such cases are more common than is, perhaps, generally supposed or at least admitted; *ergo*, the fault is not *always* on the side of the prisoners, and furnishes another proof, if another were necessary for doing away with the white slavery, – called Transportation . . .'

The letter goes on to describe an altercation between a farmer's wife and a convict servant and ends with the writer being shocked by the language used by the farmer's wife. So shocked,in fact, that he/she was about to report her, 'just to let people see how many of the unfortunate prisoners (especially women) are treated by persons permitted to have passholders, but who do not know how to behave to them properly.'

Many ballads were written with a warning, usually in the last verse:

My country men take warning e'er too late,
Lest you should share my hard unhappy fate;
Altho' but little crimes you have done,
Consider seven or fourteen years to come.
Now young men with speed your lives amend,
Take my advice as one that is your friend;
For tho' so slight you make of it while you are here,
Hard is your lot when once you get there.

For those involved in any way with transportation, it cannot have been a pleasant experience. Many ordinary people were against such a system and felt themselves and families to be tainted in some way if connected to it.

Such were feelings that when the story broke in north Wales that Edward Williams of Pen y Maes, Caernarvon had been tried and convicted in London and sentenced to be transported, his mother felt the need for a public denial of such falsehoods in the *Caernarvon Herald* of 12 April 1834. A solicitor was instructed to enquire about the truth of the matter and 'cheerfully' reported that the young man in question was a law-abiding, hard-working shop assistant.

In 1850, a convict ship with a cargo of Irish prisoners on board was sent from Britain to the Cape of Good Hope but was refused landing permission. It was forced to sail on to Van Diemen's Land. Such was the ill-feeling when it arrived that a society to abolish transportation was founded. Amongst the membership were representatives of all aspects of the community. All were agreed that transportation and the evils resulting from it should be brought to an end. The last convict-carrying ship to Van Diemen's Land was the *St. Vincent* of Spithead which sailed on 17 January 1853 and arrived at Hobart on 26 May. With the abandonment of transportation and the start of a new era, Van Diemen's Land changed its name to Tasmania.

The last prisoner-carrying ship was the *Hougoumont* (named after one of the farms on the site of the Battle of Waterloo) which sailed in 1867 from London with a cargo of Irish prisoners (Fenians – Catholic nationalists from Ulster) on board to Western Australia.

When transportation ceased, Australia became a land of where many more settlers went to of their own free will rather than by force. The families of many of the transportees have, for many years, refused to acknowledge the part played in the history of Australia by their forefathers and it is only recently that their silence has been broken. Babette Smith is convinced that Australia has suffered a major distortion of the convict history and from an obvious desire to avoid the subject. Even in 1988, at the time of the Australian Bicentenary celebrations, the only direct mention of the transportation system was by Charles, Prince of Wales. It had been ignored to a great extent by official and academic Australia and it is thanks to many a family historian that the real story has come to light. Were it not brought out into the open, an integral part of the history of one of the world's major countries would become forgotten. As well as in Australia, convict history has also been neglected in the United Kingdom until fairly recently. The stories of all convicts and their roots need to be told, remembered and appreciated. It may well be to everyone's benefit to remember the words of Coultman Smith:

South East Australia was sure to have been colonized in any event. But [the colonisation] would have failed had it not been for the substantial help, indeed a certain measure of pioneer heroism, on the part of those wretched men and women who went out to Australia in chains.

167

APPENDIX 1

Details of some convict transport ships to Australia

Name of ship	Built	Wt.	Type	Master	Surgeon	Sailed from	Embarked	Arrived	Days on journey	Numbers
Augusta Jessie	Sunderland, 1834	390 tons	Barque	J. C. Edenborough	William Leyson	London	16 August 1838	Hobart, 6 December 1838	114	210 males, 1 died on journey
Aurora (1)	Chittagong, 1817	550 tons	Ship	James Gilbert	Andrew Henderson	The Downs	27 June 1836	Hobart	102	210 males, 1 died on journey
Aurora (2)	Sunderland 1843	536 tons	Fast and sea-worthy	Valentine Ryan	W.B.Jones	London	26 April 1851	Hobart, 10 August 1851	106	229 males, 3 died on journey
Bienheim	Jarrow	375 tons	Barque	T. L. Speed	George Birnie	Woolwich	15 April 1837	Hobart, 10 July 1837	86	210 males, 6 died on journey
Britannia		520 tons	Ship	Thomas Mellvile		Portsmouth	27 March 1791	New South Wales	210	150 male + female, 21 died on journey
Brothers	Whitby	425 tons	Ship	Charles Motley	James Hall	The Downs	6 December 1823	Sydney + Hobart	153	89 females
Duchess of Northumberland	Sunderland	541 tons	Barque	George Mitchell	Charles Smith	Woolwich	27 November 1852	Hobart, 21 April 1853	144	219 females, 3 died on journey
Earl of Liverpool	Lymm	229 tons	Brig	F. B. Manning	David Thomson	London	3 December 1830	Sydney, 5 April 1831	123	90 females, 1 re-landed, 1 died on journey
Edwin Fox	Calcutta	892 tons	East Indiaman	Joshua Ferguson	Samuel Donelly	Plymouth	26 August 1858	Freemantle, 20 November 1858	86	280 males
Emma Eugenia (previous name Colonist)	Whitby	383 tons	Barque	Giles Wade	Robert Wylie	Portsmouth	6 November 1838	Port Jackson, 9 February 1838	95	200 males, 1 died on journey

Ship	Built	Tons	Type	Master	Surgeon	Departure	Departure date	Arrival		Notes
Garland Grove	Isle of Wight	433 tons	Barque	William B. Forward	William Bland	Woolwich	September 1842	Hobart, 20 January 1843	110	191 females, 1 re-landed, 1 died on journey
General Hewart	Calcutta	973 tons	Merchant man 3 decks	Percy Earl	Richard Hughes	Woolwich	26 August 1813	Sydney, 7 February 1814	165	200 males, 34 died on journey
George III	Thames	394 tons	Ship	William Hall Moxey	David Wyse	The Downs	12 December 1834			
Indispensible	France	351 tons	Brig	Henry Best	William Evans		2 March 1809	Sydney, 18 August 1809	169	62 females, 1 died on journey
Jupiter	Chepstow	347 tons	Barque	W. J. Clarke	Archibald Ferguson	The Downs	7 January 1833	Hobart, 28 May 1833	141	167 males, 4 died on journey
Lord Raglan	Cardiff	756 tons	Ship	Thomas Hybert	John Bower	Plymouth	5 March 1858	Freemantle, 1 June 1858	88	270 males, 2 died on journey
Marquis of Hastings	London	452 tons	Ship	Henry I. Naylor	Edward Jeffrey	Portsmouth	17 March 1839	Hobart, 23 July 1839	104	240 males, 7 died on journey
Midas	Hull	430 tons	Ship	James Baigrie	James Maurice	Plymouth	16 October 1826	Sydney, 15 January 1827	91	148 males, 3 died on journey
Minden	Sunderland	916 tons	Ship – teak	R. D. Crawford	John Gibson	Plymouth	21 July 1851	Swan River Colony, W.A, 14 October 1851	85	302 males, 1 died on journey
Nile	Newcastle	322 tons	Ship	James Sunter	Joseph Hislop	Spithead	21 June 1801	Sydney, 12 December 1801	176	96 females
Pyrenees	Sunderland	832 tons	Ship	B. Freeman	John Bower	England	2 February 1853	Freemantle, 30 April 1853	87	296 males, 3 died on journey
Sea Park	Northumberland	835 tons	Ship	Thomas Speeding	Josiah Caldwell	London	1 January 1851	Freemantle, 5 April 1851	94	305 males, 1 died on journey
Sultana	Sunderland	763 tons	Ship	W. Johnson		Plymouth	29 May 1859	W.A, 19 August 1859	83	224 males

APPENDIX 2

Other ships that took convicts from north Wales to Australia:

America: a rather ironic name for an Australia-bound ship. During voyage, dysentery broke out: fifty men suffered, resulting in seven deaths on board ship and another two in hospital after arrival.

Amphitrite, Augusta Jessie (2nd voyage), *Aurora 1* and *2*

Britannia: sailed as one of the 'The Third Fleet', in company of *Active, Admiral Barrington,* and *Albemarle Brothers*

Cadet: an Isle of Man built ship in 1841, barque rigged, weighing 465 tons. She had a mortality rate of 1 death per 21.7 convicts, i.e. 7 out of 159 males died on voyage!

Duchess of Northumberland: carried the last contingent of female convicts for Van Diemen's Land.

Dudbrook

Elizabeth & Henry

Emma Eugenia

Experiment: sailed via Cowes and Rio de Janeiro.

Fanny: cholera broke out on board ship before she set sail.

Friendship: did not sail well. Lost nineteen out of 133 male convicts; landed 114 at Sydney.

General Hewart

George Hibbert

Harmony

Henry: a 386 tons ship built in Quebec in 1819.

Henry Wellesley

Indispensible

Jupiter

Lady of the Lake: cost of hire = £5 19s per ton.

Layton

Maria

Marquis of Hastings

Mary

Mary Ann

Matilda: on the voyage, nine convicts were lost between England and the Cape of Good Hope and another twelve in the Southern Ocean – a rate of 1 death per 7.1 convicts.

Midas

Minden

Moffat

Morley: introduced Whooping Cough to Sydney by not declaring an outbreak on board ship.

Nautilus

Neptune

New Grove: George Rowe (surgeon) died at Scilly Islands and David Thomson was hired as a replacement.

Numa

Persian: a Quebec built(1825), 399 tons ship.

Platina

Prince of Wales: member of 'First Fleet' ; Thames built (1786) ship of 333 tons.

Princess Charlotte

Racehorse

Saint Vincent

Surrey

Sovereign

Tory

Wanstead: a cargo of 120 females; one of whom was relanded and two died during the voyage. 117 landed at Sydney.

Westmoreland

William Bryan: deaths on voyage = 1 per 18.5 prisoners.

William Pitt: outbreak of smallpox on board ship but only 1 death due to illness

York

Some of the ships that took convicts to Western Australia:

Name of ship	Built	Weight	Type	Master	Surgeon	Sailed from	Embarked	Arrived	Days on journey	Numbers
Adelaide	Calcutta	640 tons	Ship	M. Longman	S. Donnelly	Portland	19 April 1855	WA 18 July 1855	90	260 males, 1 died on journey
Dudbrook	Dundee	601 tons	Barque	John Innes	Charles K. Kevern	Plymouth	22 November 1852	WA, 7 February 1853	77	230 males, 1 re-landed, 1 died on journey
Edwin Fox	Calcutta	892 tons	Ship	Joseph Ferguson		Plymouth	26 August 1858	WA	86	280 males
Merchantman	Sunderland	1018 tons	Ship	William Gardiner	William Smith	Portland	1 July 1864	WA	73	191 males
Norwood	Sunderland	786 tons	Ship	Frank Bristow	William Sanders	Portland	18 April 1867	WA	86	254 males, 1 died on journey
Pyrenees	Sunderland	832 tons	Ship	B. Freeman	John Bower	England	2 February 1853	WA, 30 April 1853	87	296 males, 3 died on journey
Racehorse	Jersey	1079 tons	Ship	Malcolm Green	William Crauford	Portland	30 September 1865	WA	76	280 males, 2 died on journey
Ramillies	Sunderland	757 tons	Barque	Charles Hodder	Daniel Ritchie	London	20 May 1858	WA	79	280 males, 1 re-landed, 1 died on journey
Scindian	Sunderland	650 tons	Barque	James Connell	John Gibson	Portsmouth	4 March 1840	WA	89	75 males
Sea Park	Northumber-land	835 tons	Ship	Thomas Speeding	Josiah Caldwell	London	1 January 1851	Freemantle, 5 April 1851	94	304 males
Sultana	Sunderland	763 tons	Ship	W. Johnson		Plymouth	29 May, 1859	WA, 19 August 1859	83	224 males
William Jardine	Liverpool	671 tons	Ship	James Raiff	James Donnet	Plymouth	3 May, 1852	WA	88	212 males

NUMBER OF CONVICTS FROM WELSH COUNTIES
ON 'SECOND FLEET' TO BOTANY BAY.

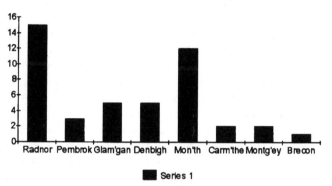

Series 1

NUMBER OF CONVICTS FROM WELSH COUNTIES
ON 'THIRD FLEET' TO BOTANY BAY.

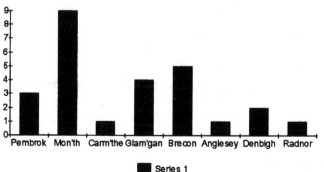

Series 1

APPENDIX 4

Terms that would have been learned by convicts

Assizes   court under the supervision of a judge but where guilt was decided by a jury. It was here that the most serious offences were tried e.g. murder, violent offences etc.

Fetters   iron hoops fitted around the ankles connected to a longer chain

Larceny   stealing someone else's property. ('Grand' and 'petty larceny' meant stealing property worth more, or less, than a shilling's worth)

Launched into eternity   a hanging

Screw   prison warder. (In the 1840s, in Pentonville Prison a device named The Crank was used to punish prisoners by which they had to turn a crank handle at least twenty times per minute or ten thousand times a day. If the set target was easily reached warders could turn a screw to make the work that much harder – from which developed an insulting name for the one who actually turned the screw and, eventually, any prison warder.)

Wearing the broad arrow   wearing a prison uniform.

Other terms were learnt on arrival e.g.:

Blue men   the police

Cat   Cat o' nine tails. (Leather whip, split into nine knotted strips. In the expression 'No room to swing a cat' – the 'cat' in question was the whip.)

Crows   derogatory term, used by the English, for local inhabitants and especially Aborigines

Currency   children = hope for the future

Factory   workplace for quarrelsome and troublesome female prisoners

The Three Legged Mare/	
The Fatal Tree/	
The Gallows Tree	on which capital punishment was carried out
Ticket of Leave	allowed a measure of freedom for prisoners and, if granted, an opportunity to look for work but not to leave any particular area without permission

Some expressions became part of Australian English and some are still used today e.g.:

cobber	a friend
jackfruit	a young man sent to gain experience on a farm (from the Aboriginal for 'a wandering white man')
larrikin	a mischievous child
manchester	bed and bathroom linen
sheila	woman
swagman	tramp or itinerant traveller

And there are some who have no memorial,
who have perished as though they had not lived;
they have become as though they had not been born,
and so have their children after them.

Ecclesiasticus, Chapter 44, verse 9